Across Borders
Preparing for Study Abroad

Kazushige Tsuji

Setsu Tsuji

Masumi Tahira

Anita L. Aden

Margaret M. Lieb

SANSHUSHA

音声ダウンロード＆ストリーミングサービス（無料）のご案内

https://www.sanshusha.co.jp/text/onsei/isbn/9784384335286/

本書の音声データは、上記アドレスよりダウンロードおよびストリーミング再生ができます。ぜひご利用ください。

Download

Streaming

写真提供

Chapter 1 　©shutterstock.com/Monkey Business Images
Chapter 2 　©iStockphoto.com/Andrea Preibisch
Chapter 3 　©iStockphoto.com/narvikk
Chapter 5 　©iStockphoto.com/jreika
Chapter 6 　©iStockphoto.com/RiverNorthPhotography
Chapter 8 　©shutterstock.com/Prostock-studio
Chapter 9 　©iStockphoto.com/babyblueut
Chapter 10 ©shutterstock.com/Daniel Hoz
Chapter 11 ©shutterstock.com/fizkes
Chapter 12 ©shutterstock.com/G.MARTYSHEVA
Chapter 15 ©iStockphoto.com/Frankhuang

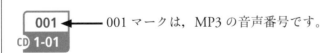
001 マークは，MP3 の音声番号です。

＊教室用として，通常のオーディオ機器で再生可能な CD（2枚組）のご用意がございます。Chapter 8 の **②** から Disc 2 になります。

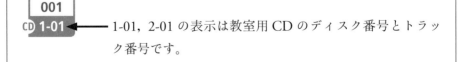
1-01，2-01 の表示は教室用 CD のディスク番号とトラック番号です。

はじめに

　グローバル化が加速する社会経済において，異文化体験を有し英語力を備えたグローバル人材を育成することは，現在の日本にとって重要な課題であり，海外留学の果たす役割は大変大きなものです。

　本テキストを通して，学習者は海外留学の準備から帰国後の対応に至る一連の流れを理解し，さまざまなシチュエーションで求められる語彙や英語表現を習得することができます。また，海外の人たちと交流する際に大切である異文化に関する基礎知識を身につけることもできます。さらに，巻末に用意した Extra Exercises により，各章に関連した実用的な知識を深めることも可能です。

　なお，本テキストは三修社から発刊の『Study Abroad! 海外語学研修のための英語と知識』と『Go! Global－Preparing for ESL Courses Abroad グローバルキャリアをめざして－語学留学のためのファーストステップ』を元に，留学準備に役立つ内容をより広くカバーするためチャプター数を増やし，取り挙げる場面を今日に即したものに改めました。これにより，これからの海外留学に役立つテキストとしてまとめられています。

　本テキストでの学びが，みなさんの海外留学を充実したものにすることを願ってやみません。そして，多くの人たちが留学を通して，グローバルキャリアへの弾みをつけ，それぞれが活躍されることを期待したいと思います。

著者一同

各章における練習問題の構成

① Dialog 1
Expand your vocabulary

会話に出てくる語句の練習問題：各語の意味の確認，発音練習，日本語から英語への変換練習

Enhance your communication skills

会話は Part 1，Part 2 から構成
Part 1： True or False 問題，会話の聞取り穴埋め問題，リピーティング，ロールプレイングなどの会話練習
Part 2： 文章の整序問題，リピーティング，ロールプレイングなどの会話練習

② Reading
Elevate your knowledge

各テーマに沿った英文読解問題：文章完成問題，英問英答問題，完成した英文のシャドーイング，英文のリピーティング

③ Dialog 2
Expand your vocabulary

応用の会話等に出ている語句の練習問題：各語の意味の確認，発音練習，日本語から英語への変換練習

Enhance your communication skills

応用の会話等の問題：選択肢問題，ディクテーション，シャドーイング

※巻末には，各章ごとに Extra Exercises が用意されています。

CONTENTS

Choosing the Destination

留学先の決定

マヤはもっと本格的に英語を学びたいと思っています。自分の目標にあった留学先を探しているところです。

Expand your vocabulary

001
CD 1-01 **1** Listen to and repeat each word. Match the English words to the Japanese words.

1.	specific	( )	a.	利用可能な
2.	destination	( )	b.	（値段が）手ごろな
3.	available	( )	c.	特定の
4.	interest	( )	d.	関心
5.	tuition fee	( )	e.	目的地
6.	reasonable	( )	f.	授業料

002
CD 1-02 **2** Listen to the Japanese words and say each one in English.

Enhance your communication skills

PART 1　マヤは学内の留学センターを訪れ，留学カウンセラーに声をかけます。

003
CD 1-03 **1** Listen to Part 1 and circle T for true or F for false for each of the following statements.

1. Maya wants to learn English for business purposes.	T / F
2. Maya went to Vancouver to study abroad last year.	T / F
3. Maya is planning to enroll in a one-month program.	T / F

2 Listen to Part 1 again and fill in the missing words.

(M : Maya, C : Study Abroad ■ Counselor)

M : Hello. Can I get ①(　　　　)(　　　　) about study abroad programs?

C : Sure. There are a lot of good places for studying abroad. Do you have a ②(　　　　) type of program ③(　　　　)(　　　　)?

M : Well... I've been thinking about learning business English.

C : Okay. How about the ④(　　　　) and the ⑤(　　　　) of stay?

M : I'd like to go to the United States or Canada. One of my friends studied abroad in Vancouver last year, and she really enjoyed her program.

C : So, shall we ⑥(　　　　)(　　　　) the West Coast of North America?

M : That ⑦(　　　　) good.

C : How about the length of stay ■ ?

M : It ⑧(　　　　)(　　　　) the cost.

C : I see. Let's ⑨(　　　　)(　　　　) what programs are ⑩(　　　　) for you.

---

3 Repeat the conversation.

4 Maya's part is missing. Listen to the conversation and speak as Maya.

5 The Study Abroad Counselor's part is missing. Listen to the conversation and speak as the Study Abroad Counselor.

6 Role play in pairs.

Check-up

■ 「海外留学」という意味。

■ 「滞在期間」という意味。「留学期間」というときは study abroad period ということもできる。

PART 2 マヤの希望を聞いて，留学カウンセラーが提案しています。

1 Put the words in parentheses in the correct order.

After accessing a computer to look up study abroad programs.

C ： Please take a look. There are quite a few **3** courses that match your interests **4** .

M ： Do you have any suggestions for a good English business program?

C ： Actually, I think this program ① (a / be / you / good / match / for / would). _____

M ： Oh, what do you like about it?

C ： You can ② (as / practical / well / learn / business / skills) as English. _____

M ： That sounds perfect since I hope to work at a global company someday.

C ： In addition, ③ (it / fees / reasonable / has / tuition). _____

M ： Let me see. I agree, it does look affordable **5** .

2 Repeat the conversation.

3 Maya's part is missing. Listen to the conversation and speak as Maya.

4 The Study Abroad Counselor's part is missing. Listen to the conversation and speak as the Study Abroad Counselor.

5 Role play in pairs.

Check-up

3 「かなり多数の」という意味。

4 「あなたの関心に合う」という意味。match の代わりに fit with や suit などを使うこともできる。

5 「値段が手ごろな」という意味。reasonable, inexpensive, fair などに言い換えることができる。「値段が高い」は，expensive, costly, pricey などの表現がある。

Elevate your knowledge

海外留学に出発するまでにはさまざまな準備が必要なため，時間を要することもあります。下記は，留学準備についての助言です。

1 Read the following passage and fill in the blanks with the appropriate words from the choices below.

Preparation for study abroad ① (　　　　) of gathering information and making ② (　　　　) decisions. Although agencies help with some of these decisions for successful ③ (　　　　) studying, students should think about future jobs or personal ④ (　　　　) on their own. In addition, it takes time to get all the ⑤ (　　　　) ready. It is important to use time wisely ⑥ (　　　　) waiting for results; therefore, students should make an effort to continue ⑦ (　　　　) their English skills in order to ⑧ (　　　　) their preparation time.

■選択肢■ while | overseas | documents | consists | informed | expectations | maximize | improving

Notes 海外に渡航する際に必要な手続きの代表として査証 visa の取得がある。査証は，ある国に入国・滞在を希望する人が，その国の大使や領事によって入国を許可されていることを証明してもらうこと，またその証明印のことを指す。査証発給の基準は各国で異なり，一定期間以下の滞在や，留学や観光の渡航目的によって不要となる場合も多い。

2 Answer the questions about the passage.

1. What can agencies help students do?

_____

2. What do students need to think about before studying abroad?

_____

3. What advice is given on how to make good use of the preparation time?

_____

3 Listen to the passage and shadow the speaker's voice.

4 Repeat the three sentences you hear.

Expand your vocabulary

011
CD 1-11 **1** **Listen to and repeat each word. Match the English words to the Japanese words.**

1. participate in ( )   a. （法的に）有効な
2. apply for ( )   b. 発行する
3. valid ( )   c. 提出する
4. admission ( )   d. 入学許可
5. submit ( )   e. ～に申し込む
6. issue ( )   f. ～に参加する

012
CD 1-12 **2** **Listen to the Japanese words and say each one in English.**

Enhance your communication skills

留学先を決めたマヤに，留学カウンセラーが手続きについて説明しています。

013
CD 1-13 **1** **Listen to the conversation and choose the most appropriate answer.**

1. **What will Maya probably do next?**
   a. Take a test to evaluate her English fluency.
   b. Apply for a visa to the US.
   c. Write a message requesting an application to the program.
   d. Reserve a plane ticket to San Francisco.

2. **Which is true about a US visa?**
   a. Maya does not have to apply for it.
   b. Maya must renew her passport before applying for it.
   c. Maya needs it before applying for a study abroad program.
   d. Maya can apply for it online.

3. **What does Maya ask the counselor to do?**
   a. To teach her how to apply for a US visa.
   b. To apply for a program on her behalf.
   c. To correct her application after she completes it.
   d. To inform her of the arrival of the admission letter.

2 Listen to the conversation again and complete the sentences.

（C：Study Abroad Counselor, **M**：Maya）

C ： So, have you decided on a study abroad program?

M ： Yes, ① _____ the program at San Francisco Griffith University. What do I need to do next?

C ： First of all, ②_____ the program. You can do that on its website.

M ： I also need to apply for a student visa to the US, right?

C ： Definitely. Do you have a valid passport?

M ： Yes. I already got it last year.

C ： OK. You need it for the visa application; however, you need ③ _____ _____ to the program first.

M ： So, ④_____ the acceptance letter before applying for the US visa?

C ： That's right. Also, for your information, the visa application ⑤_____ _____ .

M ： Great! When do you think the admission letter ■ ⑥_____ ?

C ： Usually, it takes a few weeks.

M ： I see. Would you be willing to■ check my application form after I complete■ it?

C ： Yes, I'd be happy to■ help you.

M ： Thank you.

C ： You're welcome. Good luck with your application!

3 Listen to the conversation and shadow the speakers' voices.

> **Check-up**
> ■ 「入学許可証・合格通知書」という意味で, letter of acceptance ということもある。便宜上 letter の語を使っているが, e メールなどを通じてデジタル文書で受け取ることが一般的になっている。
> ■ 「～していただいてもかまわないでしょうか」という意味。丁寧に依頼する際の表現。
> ■ 「(様式に) 記入する」という意味。fill in や fill out と言い換えることもできる。
> ■ 「喜んで～する」という意味で, 相手の申し出を快諾する際の表現。I'd は I would の省略形。I'd love to do. や, より丁寧な I'd be pleased to do. などの表現もよく使われる。

2

On the Plane

飛行機内にて

マヤは初めて海外英語研修に参加することになりました。日本から目的地に向かって出発します。

1

Expand your vocabulary

 014
CD 1-14

1 Listen to and repeat each word. Match the English words to the Japanese words.

1.	boarding pass	( )	a.	肌寒い	
2.	aisle	( )	b.	頭上の	
3.	overhead	( )	c.	搭乗券	
4.	airsick	( )	d.	通路	
5.	turbulence	( )	e.	飛行機に酔った	
6.	chilly	( )	f.	乱気流	

015
CD 1-15

2 Listen to the Japanese words and say each one in English.

Enhance your communication skills

PART 1 マヤは，アメリカに向かうため国際便に乗り込みました。マヤと客室乗務員の会話です。

016
CD 1-16

1 Listen to Part 1 and circle T for true or F for false for each of the following statements.

1. Maya is going to be seated close to the window.　　　　　　　　　　T / F

2. Maya pressed the call button because she has a headache.　　　　　T / F

3. Maya needs to remain in her seat until the FASTEN SEATBELT sign is turned off.

　　　　　　　　　　　　　　　　　　　　　　　　　　　　　　　　T / F

2 Listen to Part 1 again and fill in the missing words.

(M : Maya, F : Flight Attendant **1**)

M : Excuse me. Could you help me? There is someone ① (   )(   )
(   ) seat. This is my ② (   )(   ).

F : ③ (   ). Actually, your seat is ④ (   ). That is a ⑤ (   )
(   )**2**. The other passenger is in the ⑥ (   ) seat.

M : I understand. Thank you.

F : You're welcome. Can I help you with anything else?

M : Yes, could you help me put my bag in the ⑦ (   )(   )**3**, please?

F : Of course.

M : Thank you very much.

F : If you need more help, please press the CALL button on the ⑧ (   )
above you.

Shortly after the plane takes off, Maya presses the call button.

M : Excuse me. I'm feeling a bit airsick**4**.

F : Oh, I'm sorry to hear that. There was a lot of turbulence during the take off.

M : Would it be okay for me to go to ⑨ (   )(   )?

F : Sorry, you need to stay in your seat until the captain ⑩ (   )
(   ) the FASTEN SEATBELT sign.

M : Okay.

F : I will come back to check on you later.

M : That's very kind of you. Thanks.

016
1-16
017
1-17
018
1-18

3 Repeat the conversation.

4 Maya's part is missing. Listen to the conversation and speak as Maya.

5 The Flight Attendant's part is missing. Listen to the conversation and speak as the Flight Attendant.

6 Role play in pairs.

Check-up
1 「客室乗務員」のこと。cabin attendant とも言う。
2 「窓側席」のこと。「通路側席」は aisle seat と言う。
3 「座席上部にある荷物を入れる棚」のこと。Would/Could you help me with my bag? などとも言える。ジャケットなどは預けることもできる。
4 「飛行機酔い」は airsickness あるいは motion sickness と言う。

PART 2 マヤは客室乗務員に何か頼んでいます。

1 **Put the words in parentheses in the correct order.**

The flight attendant checks on Maya.

F : How are you feeling? ① (something / I / get / drink / to / shall / you)?

M : Yes, could I have a glass of orange juice, please **5** ?

F : Sure.

M : And I feel a little chilly. ② (wonder / I / bring / blanket / you / me / could / another / if)?

F : OK. I'll be right back. ... Here you are, some orange juice and a blanket.

M : Great! Thank you very much.

F : My pleasure. That's what I'm here for. ③ (me / if / you / know / else / need / let / anything).

M : OK, thank you.

 2 **Repeat the conversation.**

 3 **Maya's part is missing. Listen to the conversation and speak as Maya.**

 4 **The Flight Attendant's part is missing. Listen to the conversation and speak as the Flight Attendant.**

5 **Role play in pairs.**

Check-up

5 機上では，beverage（水以外の飲み物）は原則無料であるが，国内線やアメリカ系の航空会社ではアルコール類は有料である。ただし，格安航空会社ではすべての beverage が有料である。また機内は気圧の加減で酔いが回りやすい。

Elevate your knowledge

国際線は飛行が長時間に及ぶので, 体調変化などを含むさまざまな状況が起こりえます。下記は, 渡航時に機内で発生することがある症状とそれを防ぐための留意点です。

1 **Read the following passage and fill in the blanks with the appropriate words from the choices below.**

Air travel is ① (　　　　　　　) to anyone traveling ② (　　　　　　　). This is particularly true for students ③ (　　　　　　　) in overseas English programs. Although ④ (　　　　　　) offer different seating categories, students usually fly economy to get to their ⑤ (　　　　　). In the case of ⑥ (　　　　　　), many passengers today may show ⑦ (　　　　　) of "economy class syndrome." In order to ⑧ (　　　　　　) its effects, they should wear loose clothing, do some stretches, and drink plenty of water on an airplane.

選択肢 airlines | destinations | symptoms | essential | counterbalance | long distances | long haul flights | participating

Notes 「エコノミークラス症候群」の正式名は「深部静脈血栓症」(deep vein thrombosis) である。空気が乾いている飛行機の中で, 長時間座席に同じ姿勢で座ったままでいることで, 静脈の血が流れにくくなり血の固まりができる病気。重症の場合は命を落とすこともある。実際にはビジネスクラスやファーストクラス, また鉄道や車でも起きるため, 今では「旅行血栓症」(travel thrombosis) と呼ばれている。

2 **Answer the questions about the passage.**

1. What kind of seating are students most likely to have on a plane?

_____

2. These days, what concerns do some passengers have on long haul flights?

_____

3. How can passengers prevent "economy class syndrome"?

_____

3 **Listen to the passage and shadow the speaker's voice.**

4 **Repeat the three sentences you hear.**

Expand your vocabulary

1 **Listen to and repeat each word. Match the English words to the Japanese words.**

1.	last	( )	a.	締める
2.	fasten	( )	b.	控える
3.	in accordance with	( )	c.	延期する
4.	refrain	( )	d.	続く
5.	postpone	( )	e.	開始する
6.	commence	( )	f.	〜に従って

2 **Listen to the Japanese words and say each one in English.**

Enhance your communication skills

機内ではパイロットや客室乗務員などから，さまざまなアナウンスがあります。マヤが搭乗中の飛行機でもアナウンスがありました。

1 **Listen to the announcements and choose the most appropriate answer.**

1. **What is the first announcement about?**
   a. It is about a smooth flight.
   b. It is about how to use the restroom.
   c. It is about upcoming turbulence.
   d. It is about a flight delay.

2. **How long must passengers remain in their seats?**
   a. For a long time.
   b. For 15 minutes.
   c. Until the seat belt sign is turned off.
   d. Until another announcement is made.

3. **According to the second announcement, what will the flight attendants be doing shortly?**
   a. They will be serving dinner.
   b. They will be selling duty-free items.
   c. They will be seated for their own safety.
   d. They will bring pamphlets to passengers.

2 **Listen to the announcements again and complete the sentences.**

ANNOUNCEMENT BY A FLIGHT ATTENDANT

May I have your attention, please? The captain has informed us that ①＿＿＿＿＿

＿＿＿＿＿＿＿＿＿＿＿＿＿＿＿＿＿ which will last for about 15 minutes.

Would you please return to your seat, make sure that your seat belt is securely

fastened, and ②＿＿＿＿＿＿＿＿＿＿＿＿＿＿＿＿＿ while the "FASTEN

SEATBELT" sign is on. In accordance with instructions from the captain,

your flight attendants will also take their seats at this time. We are afraid that

③＿＿＿＿＿＿＿＿＿＿＿＿＿＿＿＿ until after the turbulence has

passed. Thank you.

AFTER THE TURBULENCE

May I have your attention, please? ④＿＿＿＿＿＿＿＿＿＿＿＿＿＿＿＿

and you are now free to move about the cabin. However, we recommend that

⑤＿＿＿＿＿＿＿＿＿＿＿＿＿＿＿ while you are in your seat. In

a short time, we will be commencing our in-flight sales of duty-free items.

⑥＿＿＿＿＿＿＿＿＿＿＿＿＿＿＿＿ in your seat pocket for details.

Thank you.

---

3 **Listen to the announcements and shadow the speaker's voice.**

Check-up

1 「機長」(chief pilot) のこと。「副操縦士」は co-pilot。

Airport Arrival Procedures

入国手続き

アメリカに到着したマヤは空港でさまざまな手続きを行っています。

Expand your vocabulary

027
CD 1-27

1 **Listen to and repeat each word. Match the English words to the Japanese words.**

1. arrival card   ( )   a. 帰りの航空券
2. purpose   ( )   b. 〜に近い
3. sightseeing   ( )   c. ホストファミリー
4. host family   ( )   d. 目的
5. close to   ( )   e. 観光
6. return ticket   ( )   f. 入国カード

028
CD 1-28

2 **Listen to Japanese words and say each one in English.**

Enhance your communication skills

PART 1 マヤは，アメリカに到着後，まず「入国管理」に移動し，必要な書類を用意して順番を待っています。

029
CD 1-29

1 **Listen to Part 1 and circle T for true or F for false for each of the following statements.**

1. Maya is going to visit her friends in America.   T / F
2. Maya is staying in America for four weeks.   T / F
3. The family that Maya's going to stay with live at 550 Lake Merced Blvd., San Francisco.   T / F

2 Listen to Part 1 again and fill in the missing words.

(O : Officer, M : Maya)

O : Next, please. May I see your passport and ① (　　　　　)(　　　　　),
    please? ■

M : Yes, here ② (　　　　　)(　　　　　) ■ .

O : Thank you. And what's the ③ (　　　　　) of your visit to America?

M : I'm here to study English and to do some ④ (　　　　　).

O : What do you do in Japan?

M : I'm a ⑤ (　　　　　)(　　　　　).

O : I see. And ⑥ (　　　　　)(　　　　　) will you be staying in America?

M : For ⑦ (　　　　　)(　　　　　).

O : And where will you be staying?

M : I'll be staying with the Fenton family, my host family.

O : Could you tell me their ⑧ (　　　　　), please?

M : Yes. They live at ⑨ (　　　　　) Lake Merced Blvd., San Francisco, very
    ⑩ (　　　　　)(　　　　　) San Francisco Griffith University.

O : Thank you.

---

3 Repeat the conversation.

4 Maya's part is missing. Listen to the conversation and speak as Maya.

5 The Officer's part is missing. Listen to the conversation and speak as the Officer.

6 Role play in pairs.

Check-up

■ 許可を求める時は May I ... ? / Could I ... ? / Can I ... ? 何かを要求する時は Could you ... ? /
Would you ... ? / Can you ... ? / Will you ... ? などを使う。

■ 物を差し出す時に使う表現。原則ひとつの場合は，Here it is. 物を特定する場合は Here is
my passport. また，Here you are. / Here you go. も同じ意味で使われる。

IMMIGRATION

1 **Put the words in parentheses in the correct order.**

O : May I see (reservation / the / return / to / your / for / Japan), please?

M : I'm sorry, what was that?

O : Your return ticket ❸ , ② (me / please / the / for / show / your / reservation / flight) back to Japan.

M : Oh, yes, of course. Here it is.

O : Thank you. ③ (America / a / stay / in / have / nice) .

M : Thank you.

---

032 **CD1-32** **2** **Repeat the conversation.**

033 **CD1-33** **3** **Maya's part is missing. Listen to the conversation and speak as Maya.**

034 **CD1-34** **4** **The Officer's part is missing. Listen to the conversation and speak as the Officer.**

5 **Role play in pairs.**

Check-up

❸ return ticket は帰りの航空券のこと（米）。往復切符を表す場合もあるので注意が必要（英）。

Elevate your knowledge

入国の手続きには，入国審査，手荷物の受け取りや税関での審査があります。下記は，入国手続の概要です。

1 Read the following passage and fill in the blanks with the appropriate words from the choices below.

Generally, passengers are required to fill out a ① (　　　　　　　　) and an arrival card on board before ② (　　　　　　　　). Then when they arrive at their ③ (　　　　　　　　), they must follow certain ④ (　　　　　　　　). First, they must go through a passport and visa check at ⑤ (　　　　　　　　). Next, they go to the ⑥ (　　　　　　　) area and pick up their luggage. Finally, they line up for a baggage inspection at ⑦ (　　　　　　　)before they ⑧ (　　　　　　　) the airport.

選択肢 immigration control | landing | baggage claim | procedures | exit | destination | customs declaration form | customs |

Notes (1)「入国カード」は landing card, incoming passenger card, immigration form, disembarkation card などとも呼ばれる。
(2) 入国審査では citizens と non-citizens あるいは residents と non-residents に分かれる。
(3) 入国や税関の手続きは immigration officer（入国管理官），customs officer/inspector（税関吏）が行う。
(4) 手荷物受取所の「円形コンベアー」は carousel / belt。
(5) イギリス英語圏では「列に並ぶ」は queue up。

2 Answer the questions about the passage.

1. What do passengers usually have to do before landing?

   _____

2. What happens at immigration control?

   _____

3. What is the last thing passengers must do before they exit the airport?

   _____

035
1-35 **3** Listen to the passage and shadow the speaker's voice.

036
1-36 **4** Repeat the three sentences you hear.

Expand your vocabulary

1 **Listen to and repeat each word. Match the English words to the Japanese words.**

1. claim tag   (   )   a. 不便
2. locate   (   )   b. 配達する
3. place   (   )   c. 手荷物引換証
4. deliver   (   )   d. 予期しない
5. unexpected   (   )   e. 捜し出す
6. inconvenience   (   )   f. 置く

2 **Listen to the Japanese words and say each one in English.**

Enhance your communication skills

マヤは入国審査後に，航空会社に預けた荷物を受け取るために手荷物受取所へ移動しました。

1 **Listen to the conversation and choose the most appropriate answer.**

1. **What has happened to Maya?**
    a. She can't find her claim tag.
    b. She can't locate her suitcase.
    c. She has lost her carry-on bag.
    d. She has lost her way to the baggage claim.

2. **What color is her suitcase?**
    a. Silver with a green and red belt.
    b. Red with a silver and red belt.
    c. Green with a red and silver belt.
    d. Red and green with a silver belt.

3. **When will she probably get her suitcase?**
    a. At 8:00 tonight.
    b. Tomorrow before noon.
    c. Today before noon.
    d. Around 5:50 tomorrow morning.

2 **Listen to the conversation again and complete the sentences.**

(**M** : Maya,　**C** : Clerk)

In the baggage claim area

M : Excuse me, could you help me? ① _____. I've checked

the baggage claim area, but I can't find it.

C : I see. How many bags did you check in?

M : Two. Here's the claim tag **1**.

C : What does it look like **2**?

M : It is ② _____ that suitcase over there.

C : What color is your suitcase?

M : It's silver with a red and ③ _____.

C : OK, let me see if I can locate it for you.

M : Thank you very much for your help.

After a short wait

C : Your suitcase seems to have been placed onto a different flight.　As soon as it gets

here tomorrow,　④ _____ where you will be staying.

M : What a relief!　I will be staying with the Fenton family.　Their address is 550 Lake

Merced Blvd., San Francisco.

C : Got it. Thank you.

M : Around what time tomorrow ⑤ _____ **3**?

C : It should arrive at this airport at 8:00 in the morning.　Therefore,

⑥ _____ that it should get to you before noon.

M : I am glad to hear that. This is the telephone number of my host family.　If

anything unexpected happens, please call me.

C : All right. We're very sorry for the inconvenience.

3 **Listen to the conversation and shadow the speakers' voices.**

Check-up

1 「委託荷物の荷札の半券」で baggage claim tag とも言う。

2 「どのようなスーツケースですか。」という意味。What features does it have? などとも言える。

3 「スーツケースは明日の何時頃に受け取れますか。」という意味。「何時頃までに，スーツケースをこの住所に配達していただけますか。」の場合は，By what time can you have the suitcase delivered to this address? と言う。

Meeting the Host Family

ホームステイ

マヤはアメリカに到着後，迎えに来てくれたホストファーザーに会います。いよいよホームステイが始まります。

Expand your vocabulary

040
CD1-40 **1** Listen to and repeat each word. Match the English words to the Japanese words.

1. drowsy ( )   a. （ガソリンなどを）満タンにする
2. parking lot ( )   b. 詰め込む
3. squeeze ( )   c. 向かって進む
4. head ( )   d. （車を）脇に寄せて止める
5. pull over ( )   e. 眠い
6. fill up ( )   f. 駐車場

041
CD1-41 **2** Listen to the Japanese words and say each one in English.

Enhance your communication skills

PART 1 マヤはアメリカに到着後，迎えに来てくれたホストファーザーと会います。

042
CD1-42 **1** Listen to Part 1 and circle T for true or F for false for each of the following statements.

1. Mr. Fenton is going to take care of Maya as a member of the family.   T / F
2. The parking lot is not near the airport.   T / F
3. Maya was relaxed and had a good sleep on board.   T / F

2 **Listen to Part 1 again and fill in the missing words.**

(J : Jack, **M** : Maya)

J : Hello. Maya. ① (   ) to America. *(Shakes her hand.)*

M : It's nice to meet you**■**, Mr. Fenton. Thank you for having me stay with you and
your family.

J : My ② (   )**■**. I have my car parked in the ③ (   )(   ).

M : Wow, the airport is so big. Is your car ④ (   )(   ) here?

J : Not really. Can I help you with your ⑤ (   )?

M : Oh yes, thanks a lot.

J : You're welcome. How was your ⑥ (   ) to San Francisco?

M : It was OK. But, I was so ⑦ (   ) about coming to America that I couldn't
sleep well.

J : Oh, I see. You must ⑧ (   )(   )(   ) the long trip,
then.

M : Yes, I was ⑨ (   ) when we arrived at the airport. But I'm feeling great
now ⑩ (   )(   ) this beautiful sunshine.

J : Good! I'm glad to hear that.

3 **Repeat the conversation.**

4 **Maya's part is missing. Listen to the conversation and speak as Maya.**

5 **Jack's part is missing. Listen to the conversation and speak as Jack.**

6 **Role play in pairs.**

Check-up

■ 「はじめまして」は Nice to meet you. / I am glad to meet you. なども使える。

■ 「どういたしまして」は You are welcome. / Not at all. なども使える。

1 **Put the words in parentheses in the correct order.**

J : Here's my car. Hop in.

M : Thanks.

J : I'll squeeze your suitcase into the trunk **3** .

M : ① (sorry / trouble / with / I'm / to / that / you). It's pretty heavy.

J : Oh, don't worry. I can manage. Make yourself comfortable.

M : I'm sorry, I didn't hear what you said. Could you repeat that?

J : ② (just relax / I / what / meant / was / in the car). I'll be there in a second.

M : Thanks.

J : Alright. We're all set. We'll take the freeway **4** heading north.

M : ③ (is / far / it / from here / how / your place / to) ?

J : It's about a 50-minute drive to home. Oh, my car is getting low on gas **5** . I'll just pull over at a gas station to fill up.

045
1-45 **2** **Repeat the conversation.**

046
1-46 **3** **Maya's part is missing. Listen to the conversation and speak as Maya.**

047
1-47 **4** **Jack's part is missing. Listen to the conversation and speak as Jack.**

5 **Role play in pairs.**

Check-up

3 「車のトランク」のこと。イギリス英語圏では boot と言う。

4 「高速道路」。highway, expressway, motorway とも言う。

5 イギリス英語圏では，「ガソリン」のことを petrol と言う。「軽油」は diesel。

Elevate your knowledge

海外留学の場合，留学生は現地の家庭に滞在することがあります。下記は，ホームステイに関しての事前準備や心構えです。

1 Read the following passage and fill in the blanks with the appropriate words from the choices below.

When studying abroad, students often live with ① (　　　　　) families. A ② (　　　　　) gives them an excellent chance to learn about international culture and ③ (　　　　　). It also helps them improve their English language skills in a ④ (　　　　　) environment. To ensure a happy and successful homestay, students should respect and ⑤ (　　　　　) to the daily ⑥ (　　　　　) of their homestay family, while doing their best to communicate with them. They should also make the ⑦ (　　　　　) effort to ⑧ (　　　　　) out around the house.

選択肢 utmost ｜ homestay ｜ caring ｜ lifestyles ｜ adhere ｜ local ｜ help ｜ routine

Notes (1)「留学生」は，foreign という語の持つ疎外感を避けるために，foreign student ではなく international / overseas student が好まれる。
(2) 留学生の滞在を専門に扱うスタッフを accommodation officer / homestay coordinator と呼ぶ。

2 Answer the questions about the passage.

1. What are the benefits of staying with a local family?

_____

2. What should students do in order to ensure a happy and successful homestay?

_____

3. What should students make the utmost effort to do?

_____

048
01-48
3 Listen to the passage and shadow the speaker's voice.

049
01-49
4 Repeat the three sentences you hear.

Expand your vocabulary

1 **Listen to and repeat each word. Match the English words to the Japanese words.**

1. cooking utensil ( )   a. 感謝する
2. brand new ( )   b. アレルギーの
3. fridge ( )   c. 新品の
4. hesitate ( )   d. 料理器具
5. allergic ( )   e. ためらう
6. appreciate ( )   f. 冷蔵庫

2 **Listen to the Japanese words and say each one in English.**

Enhance your communication skills

アメリカに到着した次の日の朝，マヤはホストファミリーのケイとジャックに家の中を案内をしてもらっています。

1 **Listen to the conversation and choose the most appropriate answer.**

1. **Whom should Maya ask for help when having trouble with the brand-new stove?**
   a. She should ask Jack.
   b. She should ask Kay.
   c. She should ask the computer engineer.
   d. She should ask both Jack and Kay.

2. **At what time can Maya do her laundry and take a shower?**
   a. Anytime.
   b. Anytime except before 7:00 in the morning.
   c. Anytime except before 7:00 in the evening.
   d. Anytime, but only if she gets permission from Kay or Jack.

3. **Is there anything Maya cannot eat?**
   a. No, there is not.
   b. Yes, foods which contain peanuts.
   c. Yes, she loves peanuts.
   d. Yes, there are probably many dishes she cannot eat.

2 **Listen to the conversation again and complete the sentences.**

（K : Kay, M : Maya, J : Jack）

K : Good morning, Maya. How are you today? ■**1**

M : I'm feeling a lot better, thanks.

J : Did you sleep well?

M : Yes, I slept soundly ■**2** ①_____.

K : That's good. Maybe, ②_____ so that you know where things are.

M : OK, that'd be helpful. Wow, you have a beautiful, modern kitchen.

K : Oh, thank you. If you want to cook meals yourself, you can use whatever cooking utensils we have.

M : I love cooking for my family, so I hope to make something yummy for you, too.

J : And ③_____ this brand-new stove, just ask Kay to help you out. I am not very good with cutting edge technology ■**3**.

K : Come on, Jack. Don't be silly. You're a computer engineer.

M : Mrs. Fenton, can I keep food and drinks I buy in the fridge?

K : Of course. Oh, and please call me Kay. And here's the laundry room. This is the washer/dryer ■**4**. ④_____ here whenever you like.

M : Great, thank you. Also, when is a good time for me to take a shower?

K : Oh, anytime is fine. By the way, we usually sit down to dinner around 7:00. If there is anything you can't eat, don't hesitate to let me know.

M : OK, thank you. As I mentioned in my e-mail, ⑤_____, but otherwise I'm all right. Anyway, I really appreciate your consideration.

K : No problem. You're a member of our family now, so ⑥_____ _____.

3 **Listen to the conversation and shadow the speakers' voices.**

Check-up

■**1** How are you doing/feeling? とも言う。くだけた表現として How's it going? も使える。その返事として「まずまずです」は Not so/too bad, thanks. / Pretty good, thanks. などと言える。

■**2** 「ぐっすり眠る」という意味で，sleep deeply/well とも言う。

■**3** 「最先端技術」のことで state-of-the-art technology とも言う。

■**4** 「乾燥機能付き洗濯機」。

Sharing Japanese Culture

日本の文化

マヤは，お世話になるホストファミリーに日本から持ってきたおみやげを渡します。

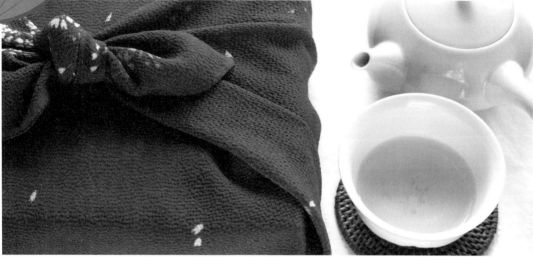

1

Expand your vocabulary

 053
CD 1-53 **1** **Listen to and repeat each word. Match the English words to the Japanese words.**

1. souvenir ( ) a. 敷く
2. represent ( ) b. 風呂用品
3. spread ( ) c. おみやげ
4. bathing article ( ) d. 利口な
5. smart ( ) e. 包む
6. wrap ( ) f. 表す

054
CD 1-54 **2** **Listen to the Japanese words and say each one in English.**

Enhance your communication skills

 PART 1 マヤはホストファミリーにおみやげを渡しているところです。まずはケイに渡しています。

055
CD 1-55 **1** **Listen to Part 1 and circle T for true or F for false for each of the following statements.**

1. Maya gave Kay something Japanese. T / F
2. Kay knew how to use the present Maya gave her. T / F
3. Maya explained the origin of the name of the present for Kay. T / F

2 Listen to Part 1 again and fill in the missing words.

(**M** : Maya, **K** : Kay, **J** : Jack)

M : I have brought some ① (　　　　　　) from Japan for you. This is for you, Kay.

K : Oh, what a ② (　　　　)(　　　　　　)! Thank you. May I open it?

M : Sure, please go ahead. I hope you like it.

K : How nice! Can you tell me what it is?

M : Sure. We call it *furoshiki*. It's a ③ (　　　　)(　　　　　　) with a print of *ukiyo-e* .

K : *Furoshiki*? Is there a ④ (　　　　)(　　　　) it?

M : Yes. *Furo* ⑤ (　　　　) bath and *shiki* means to spread.

K : That's interesting. What's it used for?

M : In the old days people carried their ⑥ (　　　　)(　　　　　　) and clothes in a *furoshiki*, and used it as a ⑦ (　　　　)(　　　　).

K : That's ⑧ (　　　　). Do you still use it in the same way?

M : No, today people use it for ⑨ (　　　) and carrying things.

K : I see.

M : Also, some people use it as an ⑩ (　　　　)(　　　　) such as a wall tapestry or tablecloth.

K : Really? How interesting. I'll use it to cover the small table in the dining room. Thank you so much for this thoughtful gift.

3 Repeat the conversation.

4 Maya's part is missing. Listen to the conversation and speak as Maya.

5 Kay's part is missing. Listen to the conversation and speak as Kay.

6 Role play in pairs.

Check-up

■ 浮世絵は，江戸時代（1603-1868）に日本独自の大衆美術として成立し，江戸末期より明治にかけ欧米へ多くの秀作が流出した。

■ 「タペストリー（壁掛け）」。

1 Put the words in parentheses in the correct order.

M ： Jack, this is for you. This is a *happi* ❸ . It's a jacket with a ① (back / character / the / Chinese / on).

J ： Wow! I've never seen anything like it. What is the significance of the Chinese character?

M ： Chinese characters are also called *kanji*. ② (word / in / the / festival / *matsuri* / *kanji* / means).

J ： Really? That's interesting. Can I try it on?

M ： Sure. ③ (hope / fits / I / it / you) all right.

J ： This is just the right size for me. Thank you very much.

M ： You're welcome. I'm glad you like it.

2 Repeat the conversation.

3 Maya's part is missing. Listen to the conversation and speak as Maya.

4 Jack's part is missing. Listen to the conversation and speak as Jack.

5 Role play in pairs.

Check-up

❸ 法被（はっぴ）は，祭りのときに人々に，あるいは職人（craftsman, skilled worker）に着用されている腰丈や膝丈の上着である。元々，江戸時代に武士が家紋（crest）を染めた法被を着用したのに始まり，職人や火消し（firefighter）が着用するようになった。

Elevate your knowledge

留学生は，ホームステイ先や学校で日本について説明を求められる場面が多くあります。下記は，留学の際に日本に関する基礎知識をつけておくことの大切さについてです。

1 Read the following passage and fill in the blanks with the appropriate words from the choices below.

In other countries, Japanese students often find themselves in ① (　　　　) where they have to talk about issues ② (　　　　) to Japan. To their ③ (　　　　), many students realize that they don't have ④ (　　　　) knowledge of such issues to explain them to their new friends. Through ⑤ (　　　　) experiences they become aware of the importance of having a good ⑥ (　　　　) of their own country's culture and ⑦ (　　　　). Therefore, it is important for them to prepare themselves for such situations to ensure a ⑧ (　　　　) overseas experience.

■ 選択肢 ■ grasp | sufficient | situations | dismay | rewarding | traditions | relative | overseas

Notes 「…について詳しい／よく理解している」は have sufficient knowledge of..., have a good grasp of..., be knowledgeable about..., be well-informed on..., be well-versed in..., have a good understanding of..., have a firm grip on... などの表現が使える。

2 Answer the questions about the passage.

1. What situation do Japanese students often find themselves in overseas?

   _____

2. What problem do many students face in this situation?

   _____

3. What can overseas experiences help students to be aware of?

   _____

3 Listen to the passage and shadow the speaker's voice.

4 Repeat the three sentences you hear.

Expand your vocabulary

063
CD 1-63 **1** **Listen to and repeat each word. Match the English words to the Japanese words.**

1. be keen on	( )	a. 地理的な
2. stretch	( )	b. 変化がある
3. crescent	( )	c. 広がる
4. vary	( )	d. ～に夢中である
5. geographical	( )	e. 三日月
6. life expectancy	( )	f. 寿命

064
CD 1-64 **2** **Listen to the Japanese words and say each one in English.**

Enhance your communication skills

ホストファミリー先のジャックが，マヤに日本について質問しています。

065
CD 1-65 **1** **Listen to the conversation and choose the most appropriate answer.**

1. **What does Japan look like geographically?**
   a. Japan extends about 2,200 miles from one end to the other.
   b. Japan consists of four main islands with 2,200 small islands.
   c. Japan is made up of 4,000 major islands.
   d. Japan has the general shape of a square.

2. **What did Maya say to Jack about Japan's climate?**
   a. Japan does not have seasonal variation.
   b. Japan has an unpredictable climate.
   c. Climate differs from region to region.
   d. Climate is not good in general.

3. **Why does Japan have the world's longest life expectancy?**
   a. Because Japan's population will exceed 125 million soon.
   b. Because many people are on diets in Japan.
   c. Because Japan's health care system is good.
   d. Because people have a poor diet.

2 Listen to the conversation again and complete the sentences.

(J : Jack, M : Maya)

J : Maya, tell me about your country.

M : Sure. What would you like to know about Japan?

J : Anything. ① _____ about Japan.

M : Where is Japan on the map?

J : The map has the United States in the middle and Japan on the far right side. Here it is.

M : You're right. I am surprised to see Japan on a different side of the map. So, ② _____ ❶ from north to south.

J : It seems to have the general shape of a crescent.

M : Yes. Japan consists of four major islands ③ _____ ❷ .

J : Wow, I had no idea that Japan was made up of so many islands.

M : This is my hometown, Kyoto. Kyoto is bordered by Osaka and Nara to the south, with the Sea of Japan to the north.

J : I see. What is the climate like in Japan?

M : Japan has a mild climate with four seasons ❸ , but the climate ④ _____ _____ .

J : I can imagine that from Japan's geographical features. So, what's the population of Japan?

M : It is approximately 125 million. You know, Japan has ⑤ _____ _____ of some 80 years.

J : Really? That's impressive! Why do you think that is?

M : I suppose it ⑥ _____ and a well-established healthcare system.

3 Listen to the conversation and shadow the speakers' voices.

Check-up

- ❶ 約 3,500 キロメートル。1 マイル≒ 1.6 キロメートル。
- ❷ 「日本列島」のことで，the Japanese archipelago と呼ぶ。
- ❸ 「温帯気候区」(the temperate zone) に属していると言われる。

6

Taking the Bus

交通機関

いよいよ英語研修を受けるためにマヤは学校への行き方を確かめなければなりません。

1

Expand your vocabulary

066
CD 1-66

1 Listen to and repeat each word. Match the English words to the Japanese words.

1. for a change of pace　（　）　　a. 方向感覚
2. scorching　　　　　　（　）　　b. 見過す
3. cross　　　　　　　　（　）　　c. 気分転換に
4. miss　　　　　　　　（　）　　d. 散歩
5. sense of direction　　（　）　　e. 渡る
6. stroll　　　　　　　　（　）　　f. 焼けつくような

067
CD 1-67

2 Listen to the Japanese words and say each one in English.

Enhance your communication skills

PART 1　マヤはジャックに学校への行き方について質問しています。

068
CD 1-68

1 Listen to Part 1 and circle **T** for true or **F** for false for each of the following statements.

1. It takes far more than 40 minutes to walk from Maya's homestay to school.

　　　　　　　　　　　　　　　　　　　　　　　　　　T / F

2. Maya wants to know the way to the bus stop.　　　　T / F

3. The bus stop is on Logan Avenue.　　　　　　　　T / F

068
1-68

2 **Listen to Part 1 again and fill in the missing words.**

(**M** : Maya, **J** : Jack)

M : Jack, do you have ① (   )(   )?■ I have a question.

J : Sure, ② (   )(   )■.

M : It seems too far to walk to school from here. So, I am thinking of taking the bus. Is this a good idea?

J : Yes, I think so. If you walk to school, it will probably ③ (   ) (   ) about 40 minutes or so.

M : I could walk to school ④ (   )(   )(   )(   )■ for a change of pace. But, I wouldn't ⑤ (   )(   ) it on a scorching■ hot day like today.

J : ⑥ (   ) would I. Also, for your own ⑦ (   ), you shouldn't walk back home in the evening.

M : Oh, I see. Is there a bus stop nearby?

J : Yes, it's only about a ⑧ (   )(   ) from here.

M : Could you tell me where it is?

J : Sure, ⑨ (   )(   ) after you leave the house and go straight for about two blocks until you come to the main road.

M : What's the name of the road?

J : Logan Avenue. Then turn right and ⑩ (   )(   ) down the road. Then, you'll see the bus stop near the library.

068
1-68
3 **Repeat the conversation.**

069
1-69
4 **Maya's part is missing. Listen to the conversation and speak as Maya.**

070
1-70
5 **Jack's part is missing. Listen to the conversation and speak as Jack.**

6 **Role play in pairs.**

Check-up

■ 「時間がありますか」という意味で，Do you have time/a moment/a second/a sec? あるいは Can you spare me a moment/a second/a sec? とも言える。

■ 「遠慮せずにどうぞ」という意味。go ahead と同じ。

■ 「たまに」の意味で，類義語には occasionally, (every) now and then/again, from time to time などがある。

■ 「酷暑の／焼けつくような」という意味で，「酷暑の日」を scorcher と言う。

1 Put the words in parentheses in the correct order.

M : Could you tell me again, which side of the road is the bus stop on?

J : It's on the right in front of the library. The bus sign is blue and yellow. You can't miss it. **5**

M : Thanks, but unfortunately ① (have / good / I / of / a / don't / direction / sense), so I'll walk to the bus stop later today.

J : OK. Actually, ② (stroll / taking / how / a / about) now? It'll give me a chance to show you around the area, too.

M : OK, that'd be really helpful. I also ③ (want / check / to / schedule / the) of buses going to the school on the weekends, too.

2 Repeat the conversation.

071 CD1-71 **3** Maya's part is missing. Listen to the conversation and speak as Maya.

072 CD1-72 **4** Jack's part is missing. Listen to the conversation and speak as Jack.

073 CD1-73 **5** Role play in pairs.

Check-up

5 「すぐに見つかりますよ」の意味。

Elevate your knowledge

海外での移動手段には，バス・タクシー・列車などがあります。目的地までの交通の便の確認や，道に迷った時の対処方法は身につけておくべきです。下記は，バス利用に関する留意点です。

1 Read the following passage and fill in the blanks with the appropriate words from the choices below.

Students generally ① (　　　　) to school using public ② (　　　　) unless they live within walking ③ (　　　　) of the school. Buses are often the most ④ (　　　　) form of transportation for students. There is probably a bus service available in the ⑤ (　　　　) of homestay families. Students should memorize their ⑥ (　　　　) to school with the help of their host families. It is also wise to keep host families' addresses and phone numbers ⑦ (　　　　), as well as telephone numbers of local taxi companies in case students get lost or ⑧ (　　　　).

■選択肢■ handy | commute | vicinity | accessible | stranded | route | distance | transportation

Notes (1)commute は「毎日通う」という意味で，「通勤する」は commute to work と言う。
(2) in the vicinity of... は「…の近くに」という意味で，in the neighborhood of ... とも言う。
(3) keep/have... handy... は「…を手元に置く」という意味。

2 Answer the questions about the passage.

1. What is the most common form of transportation for students?

    _____

2. Who can probably help students figure out how to get to school?

    _____

3. What should students have on hand in case they get lost?

    _____

074
1-74 **3** Listen to the passage and shadow the speaker's voice.

075
1-75 **4** Repeat the three sentences you hear.

Expand your vocabulary

  1 **Listen to and repeat each word. Match the English words to the Japanese words.**

1. get off   ( )   a. 乗り換える
2. further   ( )   b. 割増しで
3. jump on   ( )   c. 本当に
4. indeed   ( )   d. 飛び乗る
5. transfer   ( )   e. 降りる
6. extra   ( )   f. もっと先の

2 **Listen to the Japanese words and say each one in English.**

Enhance your communication skills

マヤは市内に買い物へ行きバスで帰宅する途中です。どうも見慣れない風景が続くので，運転手に尋ねています。

  1 **Listen to the conversation and choose the most appropriate answer.**

1. **What problem does Maya have?**
   a. She can't figure out the way to Van Ness and Market.
   b. She is on a bus that does not go to Fisherman's Wharf.
   c. She is on a bus that does not stop at 19th Avenue.
   d. She is on a bus that goes to Van Ness and Market.

2. **Based on the driver's advice, how can Maya get to Fisherman's Wharf?**
   a. Take Bus 47 and then transfer to Bus 50.
   b. Get off three stops after this one and jump on Bus 47.
   c. Take Bus 28 or 30 for Van Ness and Market and then transfer to Bus 47 or 50.
   d. Take Bus 50 for Daly City and transfer to Bus 28 toward home.

3. **When does Maya have to pay $2.30?**
   a. When she gets off Bus 28.
   b. When she gets on Bus 47 or 50.
   c. When she gets to her destination.
   d. She doesn't have to pay $2.30

078
1-78

2 **Listen to the conversation again and complete the sentences.**

(M : Maya, D1 : Driver1, D2 : Driver2)

Maya is on the bus, but she doesn't know if it will go to Fisherman's Wharf.

M : Excuse me. ① _____ Fisherman's Wharf?

D1 : No, it isn't. This is the bus for Daly City.

M : Oh, no. What should I do?

D1 : You'll have to get off at 19th Avenue and take another bus.

M : How much further is that?

D1 : It's ② _____ .

M : Could you tell me ③ _____ then?

D1 : You should take Number 28 or 30. Those buses will take you to Van Ness and Market.

M : Do I have to take another bus from Van Ness and Market?

D1 : Yes, you do. Jump on ④ _____ Fisherman's Wharf.

M : Indeed, thanks for your help. Could you ⑤ _____ ?

D1 : Don't worry ■. I'll let you know... [5 minutes later] OK, here's 19th Avenue.

M : Thanks a lot.

D1 : You're welcome. Good luck.

Maya waits for bus number 28 or 30. Bus 28 comes and she gets on.

M : Excuse me. Does this bus go to Van Ness and Market?

D2 : Yes, it does.

M : I am trying to get to Fisherman's Wharf.

D2 : OK, but you have to transfer to Bus 47 or 50 at Van Ness and Market.

M : OK, thanks. Do I have to pay ⑥ _____ ?

D2 : Sorry, yes. You'll have to pay $2.30 when you get off the bus at Fisherman's Wharf.

078
1-78

3 **Listen to the conversation and shadow the speakers' voices.**

Check-up ....

■ 「心配はいらない」 という意味で，No problem. / Not to worry. と同じ。No worries. はオーストラリア表現。

7

✈ Orientation

学校のオリエンテーション

大学のキャンパス内で，5週間にわたる語学研修が始まります。初日のオリエンテーションの日です。

1

Expand your vocabulary

 1 Listen to and repeat each word. Match the English words to the Japanese words.

1.	placement test	( )	a.	多肢選択
2.	theme	( )	b.	線を引いて消す
3.	cross out	( )	c.	割り当てる
4.	allot	( )	d.	一致
5.	agreement	( )	e.	クラス分けテスト
6.	multiple-choice	( )	f.	テーマ

2 Listen to the Japanese words and say each one in English.

Enhance your communication skills

PART 1 オリエンテーションで，英語プログラムのコーディネーターのトムから概要説明がありました。その後，質疑応答が行われています。

 1 Listen to Part 1 and circle **T** for true or **F** for false for each of the following statements.

1. The placement test consists of essay writing and an interview.　　　T / F
2. The time given for essay writing is one hour.　　　T / F
3. When a student wants to correct a mistake, he/she has to erase it.　　　T / F

2 Listen to Part 1 again and fill in the missing words.

(T : Tom (Teacher), S1 : Student 1, S2 : Student 2)

T : That's the end of the first orientation session. Are there any questions?

S1 : Yes, I have a question. What is the placement test like?

T : The test includes writing essays, an interview, and answering ① (　　　　)
　　 (　　　　)(　　　　).

S1 : Could you tell us ② (　　　　)(　　　　)(　　　　)(　　　　) about
　　 the essay writing?

T : Sure, you have to write two short essays on ③ (　　　　)(　　　　) within
　　 60 minutes.

S1 : Can we use a dictionary?

T : No, you cannot. Also, you have to write your essays ④ (　　　　)(　　　　)
　　 on the paper provided to you.

S1 : Excuse me, what do you mean by 'in ink'?

T : You can't use a pencil. If you make a mistake, please ⑤ (　　　　)(　　　　)
　　 (　　　　) and write your ⑥ (　　　　) above it.

S2 : ⑦ (　　　　)(　　　　) the interview? What does it ⑧ (　　　　) ?

T : You will be asked some questions about ⑨ (　　　　)(　　　　), such
　　 as living with a host family, trying new things, etc. The time ⑩ (　　　　)
　　 (　　　　) each student's interview is about 10 minutes.

S2 : Thanks for the extra information.

T : You're welcome. Are there any more questions?

3 Repeat the conversation.

4 The Students' part is missing. Listen to the conversation and speak as the Students.

5 Tom's part is missing. Listen to the conversation and speak as Tom.

6 Role play in pairs.

PART 2　学生たちはさらに質問をつづけています。

① Put the words in parentheses in the correct order.

S2 : Can you describe what the grammar questions are like on the test?

T : Sure, you will be tested on subject/verb agreement, sentence structure and things like that.

S2 : It sounds difficult. How long does it last?

T : It's a 60-minute multiple-choice test. Then, ① (will / for / break /we / lunch).

S1 : Are we supposed to come back to this room after lunch?

T : Yes. Your teachers will explain your English programs as well as school activities ■ and the student services ■ available to you.

S1 : Will ② (us / campus / you / around / show / the) today?

T : Yes. We will take you on a campus tour at 2:30. ③ (around / to / we / end / plan / the day / 3:00).

② Repeat the conversation.

③ The Students' part is missing. Listen to the conversation and speak as the Students.

④ Tom's part is missing. Listen to the conversation and speak as Tom.

⑤ Role play in pairs.

Check-up

■ 課外活動には次のようなものがある。visiting museums and galleries, outdoor parties, exercise classes, sports, trips to beaches, hiking in national forests

■ 大学側が提供するサービスには，次のようなものが含まれる。 on-campus medical clinic, sports recreation center, intercultural activities, academic and mental health counseling, career counseling

Elevate your knowledge

通常，語学研修の初日には，留学生を対象としたオリエンテーションが行われます。下記は，オリエンテーションの概要です。

1 **Read the following passage and fill in the blanks with the appropriate words from the choices below.**

Generally, an orientation consists of a placement test, an information session and a campus tour. The purpose is to ensure a smooth ① (   ) for students into their new ② (   ) lives. The placement test ③ (   ) students' English abilities so that they can be placed into the ④ (   ) level of classes. The information session usually ⑤ (   ) English program expectations, campus activities, and services available to students to help them ⑥ (   ) in. Finally, the campus tour helps students to ⑦ (   ) themselves with the school's ⑧ (   ), such as the location of classrooms, the school cafeteria, and more.

■選択肢■ appropriate | familiarize | transition | assesses | facilities |
outlines | settle | academic

Notes 大学のキャンパスには，banking, bookstore, cafe, gym, medical service, mail service, restaurant, tennis court などの施設がある。

2 **Answer the questions about the passage.**

1. What is the purpose of an orientation?

2. Why do students need to take a placement test?

3. What is the role of a campus tour?

087
1-87 **3** **Listen to the passage and shadow the speaker's voice.**

088
1-88 **4** **Repeat the three sentences you hear.**

Expand your vocabulary

1 Listen to and repeat each word. Match the English words to the Japanese words.

1. post ( ) a. 目標
2. e-bulletin board ( ) b. 上級の
3. objective ( ) c. 学位教育課程
4. intermediate ( ) d. 中級の
5. advanced ( ) e. 掲示する
6. degree program ( ) f. オンライン掲示板

2 Listen to the Japanese words and say each one in English.

Enhance your communication skills

プレイスメントテスト後に昼食をとり，午後に英語プログラムなどについての説明が始まりました。

1 Listen to the conversation and choose the most appropriate answer.

1. **What will be posted on the e-bulletin board?**
   a. Class levels and room numbers.
   b. Teachers' names and class levels.
   c. Room numbers and teachers' names.
   d. Class levels, teachers' names, and room numbers.

2. **What is the objective of the GE (General English) program?**
   a. To become fluent in speaking and listening in English.
   b. To study English communication skills, but not grammar.
   c. To be placed in the upper intermediate class.
   d. To improve English communication and grammar skills.

3. **What is the objective of the EAP (English for Academic Purposes) program?**
   a. To become an English teacher.
   b. To enter university in English-speaking countries.
   c. To become proficient in English.
   d. To improve TOEIC scores.

2 Listen to the conversation again and complete the sentences.

(**M** : Maya, **T** : Tom (Teacher))

M : The test was really tough for many of us. I was wondering how can we get the results?

T : We will ①_____ based on your scores. Your class levels and teachers' names will be posted on the e-bulletin board online at the school's site.

M : ②_____ as well?

T : Yes, they will, along with the textbooks you will use. Now, I'll briefly explain the English programs. Most of you are taking the General English ■ courses. The objective of the GE program is to improve your communication skills in speaking, listening, reading, and writing ③_____.

M : How many class levels do you have?

T : There are five English levels from GE1 through GE5. The GE1, GE2, and GE3 classes ④_____ as the upper-beginner, pre-intermediate, and intermediate levels. GE4 is upper intermediate and GE5 means advanced.

M : I understand there is another program called EAP ■. What is that English program for?

T : You're right, Maya. The EAP ⑤_____. This program's ⑥_____ prepare for academic studies at the university level. If you want to enter a degree program at an American university, then you should consider applying for the EAP program after completing the GE program.

 3 Listen to the conversation and shadow the speakers' voices.

Check-up

■ English for General Purposes とも呼ばれる「一般的な目的のための英語」。

■ 「学術的な目的のための英語」で，次のような内容が含まれる。listening to lectures and note-taking, planning and writing academic essays, oral presentations, group discussions, etc.

Chapter 8

Making Phone Calls & Texting

電話＆携帯メール

マヤは誰かと連絡を取る手段として主に携帯電話を利用しています。

Expand your vocabulary

 092 CD 1-92 **1** Listen to and repeat each word. Match the English words to the Japanese words.

1. call　　　　　　　　　　（　）　　a.　〜で有名である
2. hang out with　　　　　（　）　　b.　〜とうまくやる
3. get along well with　　 （　）　　c.　おそらく
4. probably　　　　　　　 （　）　　d.　電話をかける
5. eat out　　　　　　　　 （　）　　e.　外食する
6. be famous for　　　　　 （　）　　f.　〜と時を過ごす

093 CD 1-93 **2** Listen to the Japanese words and say each one in English.

Enhance your communication skills

 PART 1　マヤは急ぎの用があり，ホストマザーのケイの携帯電話にメールし、そのあとに携帯電話で話しています。

094 CD 1-94 **1** Listen to Part 1 and circle T for true or F for false for each of the following statements.

1. Maya is having lunch now.　　　　　　　　　　　　　　　　　T / F
2. Maya will go home before she goes out with her friends.　　　T / F
3. Kay does not like chicken dishes very much.　　　　　　　　　T / F

2 **Listen to Part 1 again and fill in the missing words.**

(K : Kay, M : Maya)

Text messages

M	Hello Kay.
	Hi Maya. K
M	Are you free ① (　　　　)(　　　　)?
	Sure. ② (　　　　)(　　　　) anytime. K

Calling

K : ③ (　　　　)(　　　　)(　　　　　　) at school?

M : Everything is fine. We're at lunch now and I really enjoy ④ (　　　　　)
(　　　　)(　　　　) some of my classmates.

K : Good. You seem to be ⑤ (　　　　)(　　　　)(　　　　)(　　　　)
your new friends.

M : Yeah, it's a lot of fun to have classmates from other countries. And we're thinking
of [1] ⑥ (　　　　)(　　　　)(　　　　) dinner together tonight.

K : Lovely! Good for you.

M : So, I just wanted to ⑦ (　　　　)(　　　　)(　　　　) that I probably
won't ⑧ (　　　　)(　　　　) home until late tonight.

K : Oh, I see. You have an afternoon break. What will you do before
⑨ (　　　　)(　　　　) tonight?

M : There's a nice café on campus. I think we'll go there after class. And then, we'll
⑩ (　　　　)(　　　　)(　　　　　) 'Genji', a Japanese restaurant in
Japantown.

K : Good choice. That restaurant is famous for [2] grilled [3] chicken and California
sushi rolls. I think you'll like it as much as I do.

3 **Repeat the conversation.**

4 **Maya's part is missing. Listen to the conversation and speak as Maya.**

5 **Kay's part is missing. Listen to the conversation and speak as Kay.**

6 **Role play in pairs.**

Check-up

[1] 「…することを考えている」という意味で，…be thinking about, …be planning to などとも言
える。

[2] 「…で有名である」という意味で，悪い意味で有名な場合は be notorious/infamous for... と
言う。

[3] 「焼く」にあたる表現は, grill/broil（直火で焼く）, roast（炙る）, bake（オーブンなどで焼く）
などがある。

PART 2　ケイはマヤの行き帰りの交通手段を心配しています。

1　Put the words in parentheses in the correct order.

K ： Can you ① (get / out / how /figure / there / to)?

M ： Don't worry. There's a bus going that way from the university.

K ： I see. If you need a ride **6** home after dinner, ② (me / just / a / call / give). All right?

M ： Thanks. But, I am sure ③ (find / home / I / to / manage / back / a / can/ way). I'll see you later.

K ： All right. Have a good time. Bye for now.

M ： Bye.

097
CD 1-97

2　Repeat the conversation.

098
CD 1-98

3　Maya's part is missing. Listen to the conversation and speak as Maya.

099
CD 1-99

4　Kay's part is missing. Listen to the conversation and speak as Kay.

5　Role play in pairs.

Check-up

6「…を（自動車などに）乗せる」は give... a lift/ride と言う。

50

Elevate your knowledge

病気や事故などの突発的な出来事，あるいは帰宅が遅くなることをホームステイ先へ連絡することがあります。下記は，留学先での携帯電話の利用に関する留意点です。

1 Read the following passage and fill in the blanks with the appropriate words from the choices below.

These days, ① (   ) telephones are rarely used by students. When communicating, it is ② (   ) for students to send messages by ③ (   ) or using smartphone apps. However, it is necessary to write down important phone numbers, in case of ④ (   ). In addition, it is a good idea to carry a phone ⑤ (   ) in order to avoid low ⑥ (   ) issues. Before traveling, students should prepare to buy a ⑦ (   ) card for their smartphone or contact their service ⑧ (   ) about using their smartphone outside of Japan.

■選択肢■ texting | provider | battery | common | public | SIM | emergencies | charger

Notes (1)SIM は subscriber identity module (card) の略。
(2) 充電器のことは charger と言う。

2 Answer the questions about the passage.

1. What are two ways that students communicate?

   _____

2. Why should students write down important phone numbers?

   _____

3. What do students need to do before traveling?

   _____

3 Listen to the passage and shadow the speaker's voice.

4 Repeat the three sentences you hear.

Expand your vocabulary

1 **Listen to and repeat each word. Match the English words to the Japanese words.**

1. intensive ( ) a. 思い起こさせる
2. cough ( ) b. 流行する
3. temperature ( ) c. 集中的な
4. go around ( ) d. 会う約束をする
5. remind ( ) e. 咳
6. make an appointment ( ) f. 体温

2 **Listen to the Japanese words and say each one in English.**

Enhance your communication skills

フェントンさん夫婦が出勤後，マヤは体調がすぐれないため学校へ電話をかけ，授業に行けないことを説明しています。

1 **Listen to the conversation and choose the most appropriate answer.**

1. **What is the matter with Maya?**
   a. She has no appetite.
   b. She has a slight cough.
   c. She has a headache and a bad cough.
   d. She has a high temperature.

2. **What will Maya do today?**
   a. She will watch the television news.
   b. She will attend class in the morning.
   c. She will consult with Mr. Rix as soon as possible.
   d. She will attend class in the afternoon if she feels better.

3. **What will Maya probably do if she wants to see a doctor?**
   a. Nothing, there are no doctors in the area.
   b. She will ask her homestay parents to recommend someone.
   c. She will make an appointment with the health center.
   d. She will ask a friend.

2 **Listen to the conversation again and complete the sentences.**

(C : Clerk, M : Maya)

C : Good morning. American Language Institute. May I help you?

M : Good morning. ① _____. I am taking an intensive
English course at your school. I'm in Group 4.

C : Hi Maya. ② _____ ?

M : I'm afraid I don't feel well.

C : Oh, that's too bad. What's the matter? ■

M : I have a bad cough and a slight ❷ headache.

C : ③ _____. How's your temperature?

M : I need to check it, but I know I feel chilly.

C : Oh-oh. It said on the television news this morning that the flu ❸ is going
around. ④ _____, you should see a doctor.

M : Yes, OK. Thanks. By the way, could you tell Mr. Rix that I won't be able to
go to class at least in the morning. If I feel better, I want to attend class in the
afternoon. If I don't, then I'll stay in bed all day.

C : That's a good idea. ⑤ _____ to Mr. Rix. Also, I'd like
to remind you that the university has a health center. If you wish to see a doctor
at school, you can make an appointment.

M : ⑥ _____. I have the phone numbers. I'll see how I
feel later and might see a doctor on campus.

C : OK, I hope you feel better. Take care now. Bye.

M : Thank you. Bye.

3 **Listen to the conversation and shadow the speakers' voices.**

Check-up

■ 「どうしたのですか」の意味で，What's the problem? / What's wrong? とも言える。
❷ 頭痛の症状を表すことばとして，dull (鈍い)，sharp (鋭い)，piercing (刺すような)，severe (ひどい)，throbbing (ずきずきする)，splitting (割れるような) などがある。
❸ 「インフルエンザ」のことで，influenza の短縮語。

Chapter

9 Seeking Medical Care

病気

留学中には思いがけない病気や怪我で病院にかかることがあります。ある日マヤも具合が悪くなってしまいました。

① Expand your vocabulary

 105 CD 2-06 **1** Listen to and repeat each word. Match the English words to the Japanese words.

1. dizzy   (　)   a. 熱っぽい
2. shivering   (　)   b. 液体（飲み物）
3. ache   (　)   c. 悪寒がする
4. prescription   (　)   d. 目まいがして
5. fluid   (　)   e. 痛み
6. feverish   (　)   f. 処方箋

106 CD 2-07 **2** Listen to the Japanese words and say each one in English.

Enhance your communication skills

PART 1 マヤは，授業中に気分が悪くなり，キャンパス内にある医療センターで診察をしてもらうことにしました。

 107 CD 2-08 **1** Listen to Part 1 and circle T for true or F for false for each of the following statements.

1. Maya has an awful headache.   T / F
2. Maya has been feeling sick for four days.   T / F
3. Maya will take medicine to feel better.   T / F

2 **Listen to Part 1 again and fill in the missing words.**

(M : Maya, R : Mr. Rix (Teacher), N : Nurse Jones)

M : Excuse me, Mr. Rix. I am sorry to ① (　　　　　　　) ■ , but I don't feel well.

R : Maya, ② (　　　　　)(　　　　　)(　　　　　). What's the matter?

M : I keep feeling dizzy. And I've got a ③ (　　　　　)(　　　　　).

R : Oh, you should probably go to the ④ (　　　　　)(　　　　　) on campus.
　　Do you know where it is ?

M : Yes, I remember it from our campus tour.

Maya goes to see a nurse at the Health Center.

N : You have a bit of a temperature. ⑤ (　　　　　)(　　　　　) ■ . How do
　　you feel?

M : My throat ⑥ (　　　　　). And my body ⑦ (　　　　　)(　　　　　).

N : How long have you felt this way?

M : It started the day before yesterday.

N : Does your body have any muscle ⑧ (　　　　　) or pains?

M : Yes, my head is aching, and I feel tired, too.

N : By ⑨ (　　　　　)(　　　　　) of it, I think you've got a cold.

M : What should I do?

N : I'll ask the doctor to give you a prescription for some ⑩ (　　　　　　　)
　　(　　　　　) to help you feel better.

M : Thank you, Nurse Jones.

3 **Repeat the conversation.**

4 **Maya's part is missing. Listen to the conversation and speak as Maya.**

5 **The Teacher's and the Nurse's part is missing. Listen to the conversation
and speak as the Teacher and the Nurse.**

6 **Role play in pairs.**

■ 「お話中失礼ですが」という意味。I am sorry to disturb you, but..., Excuse me/Sorry for
interrupting you, but... などの表現も使える。

■ アメリカなどのように, 華氏 (Fahrenheit) が用いられている国がある。華氏と摂氏
(Centigrade/Celsius) の換算は, F=9/5C + 32 C=5/9 (F-32)。

1 Put the words in parentheses in the correct order.

N : You should also ① (a day / take / at / for / it / home / easy) or two and drink plenty of fluids.

M : OK, I will. So, ② (serious / nothing / it's), then?

N : No, but if you still feel feverish or have a sore throat in a couple of days, please contact the doctor. ③ (can / and / an / make / call / you / appointment) or use the online reservation system, too.

M : Thank you again, Nurse Jones.

N : You're welcome. Hope you feel better soon.

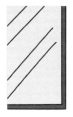

2 Repeat the conversation.

3 Maya's part is missing. Listen to the conversation and speak as Maya.

4 The Nurse's part is missing. Listen to the conversation and speak as the Nurse.

5 Role play in pairs.

Elevate your knowledge

下記は，留学期間中に体調が悪くなった場合に利用できる医療施設に関するものです。

1 Read the following passage and fill in the blanks with the appropriate words from the choices below.

Generally, universities overseas have health centers on campus with doctors and nurses ① (   ) that ② (   ) care to all students. However, the health center may be closed on weekends, so it is good for students to know where the ③ (   ) hospitals are in case of emergencies. If students have a ④ (   ) ⑤ (   ) or serious allergies, they need to share this ⑥ (   ) with their school beforehand. In any case, many overseas universities require students to take out adequate ⑦ (   ) before they ⑧ (   ) in their English programs.

選択肢 enroll | local | information | health insurance | on duty | condition | provide | medical

Notes (1) 大学内にある語学研修先の場合は，通常構内の医療センターを利用することができる。
(2) 医療通訳サービスを提供している病院もある。
(3) 観光ビザの場合，医療費は原則有料になるので，保険に入っておくことが賢明である。
(4) 大手の旅行会社は，その経験・ネットワークにより，留学先の医療機関に関する情報を有する場合がある。

2 Answer the questions about the passage.

1. What should students prepare to do in case of emergencies on the weekend?

_____

2. How can students plan ahead if they have serious medical needs?

_____

3. What do universities often require students to do before they enroll in their English programs?

_____

3 Listen to the passage and shadow the speaker's voice.

4 Repeat the three sentences you hear.

Expand your vocabulary

 1 **Listen to and repeat each word. Match the English words to the Japanese words.**

1. appetite ( )   a. 常食
2. diet ( )   b. 症状
3. symptom ( )   c. 下痢
4. stuffy nose ( )   d. 食欲
5. diarrhea ( )   e. 薬局
6. pharmacy ( )   f. 鼻づまり

 2 **Listen to the Japanese words and say each one in English.**

Enhance your communication skills

マヤは体調を崩し，ホストファミリーの近くにある病院で診察してもらうことにしました。

1 **Listen to the conversation and choose the most appropriate answer.**

1. **What is the matter with Maya?**
   a. She eats too much.
   b. She misses Japanese food.
   c. She has an upset stomach.
   d. She is upset about what she eats at her host family's home.

2. **Does Maya have any pains?**
   a. No, she doesn't.
   b. Yes, she has a constant pain in her chest.
   c. Yes, she sometimes gets a stomachache.
   d. Yes, she has pain all over her body.

3. **What are Maya's symptoms?**
   a. She sometimes gets diarrhea.
   b. She has a stuffy nose.
   c. She has a cough.
   d. She feels nauseous.

2 Listen to the conversation again and complete the sentences.

(D : Doctor Draper, M : Maya)

D : Hello, Maya. I'm Dr. Draper. ①_____ _ ?

M : I have an upset stomach, Doctor.

D : When did you start feeling sick to your stomach?

M : ②_____ , in other words, about two weeks after I arrived here from Japan.

D : I see. Have you lost your appetite?

M : Kind of, yes. Also after I eat, my stomach gets upset.

D : Can you ③_____ ?

M : No, but the diet here is different from Japan. There are many new foods that I am eating ④_____ with an American family.

D : That's understandable. Do you have any stomach pain?

M : Yes, from time to time I get a severe pain in my stomach.

D : Do you have any other symptoms ⑤_____ ?

M : Well, I did have a cough last week, and my nose isn't blocked anymore. But I still have diarrhea occasionally.

D : Do you feel nauseous?

M : I am sorry but I don't understand that word. Could you rephrase it?

D : ⑥_____ ?

M : Oh... No, I don't.

D : Well, I will give you some medicine to ease your symptoms.

M : Thank you, Doctor.

D : I'll write a prescription, and you can have it filled ■ at any pharmacy.

M : OK. I'll ask my host family to help me find a pharmacy.

D : And if you don't feel better, come back and see me.

M : OK, I will. Thanks again, Doctor.

D : You're welcome and take care, Maya.

3 Listen to the conversation and shadow the speakers' voices.

Check-up

■ 「調剤（調合）する」という意味。イギリス英語圏では，...have it made up... という表現が使われる。

Giving Presentations

プレゼンテーション

マヤのクラスでは，学生それぞれがテーマを決めて英語でプレゼンテーションを行うことになりました。

Expand your vocabulary

118
CD 2-19

1 Listen to and repeat each word. Match the English words to the Japanese words.

1. carry out   ( )   a. 明確にする
2. absolutely   ( )   b. まとめる
3. organize   ( )   c. まったく
4. findings   ( )   d. 実施する
5. proceed to   ( )   e. ～に取りかかる
6. define   ( )   f. 調査結果

119
CD 2-20

2 Listen to the Japanese words and say each one in English.

Enhance your communication skills

PART 1 マヤの今日のクラスでは，効果的なプレゼンテーションを行うための要領について話し合われています。

120
CD 2-21

1 Listen to Part 1 and circle T for true or F for false for each of the following statements.

1. The students are discussing what they should do for their presentations.   T / F
2. Topics will be given to each student by the teacher.   T / F
3. The best way to research their topics is to use the internet.   T / F

2 **Listen to Part 1 again and fill in the missing words.**

(T : Tom (Teacher), **S1** : Student 1, **S2** : Student 2)

T : Let's talk about your next assignment. How are you ① (   ) to prepare your presentation?

S1 : First, each of us has to ② (   )(   ) a topic and ③ (   ) it.

T : That's right. Tell me, how will you carry out your research[1]?

S2 : We plan to visit the library at the university to find reliable sources, such as ④ (   )(   ) or ⑤ (   ).

T : Good. And what are some other ways to ⑥ (   ) information?

S2 : We can ⑦ (   )(   )(   ) on the internet. Also, we could ⑧ (   ) interviews with other students or teachers and ask them about the topic, too.

T : You are ⑨ (   ) right[2]. What's the next ⑩ (   ) ?

S1 : After gathering information, we start writing the first draft of the presentation.

T : Yes, that's the general process of preparing for a presentation.

 3 **Repeat the conversation.**

4 **The Students' part is missing. Listen to the conversation and speak as the Students.**

 5 **The Teacher's part is missing. Listen to the conversation and speak as the Teacher.**

6 **Role play in pairs.**

Check-up

■ 「…を研究調査する」は，research..., do/conduct research into/on... と言う。
■ 賛成する場合の返事には，Yes, I agree. That's (quite) right/true. True enough. などがある。

1 Put the words in parentheses in the correct order.

T : Today's task is to organize your findings before you proceed to write them.

S1 : Proceed? What do you mean by that?

T : First, ① (define / of / presentations / you / the / your / objectives). Then, you outline them.

S2 : Professor Tom, how do you make an outline? Could you be more specific? ■

T : Sure, I'll explain more. You must be clear about ② (presentations / you'd / achieve / with / what / like / to / your).

S2 : Oh, I see. What comes next?

T : ③ (consider / you / your / audience / must). Then, you should plan the introduction, describe the main body of information with details, and prepare a summary of the topic in your conclusion.

S1 : It sounds as if giving a presentation requires a lot of time and effort.

T : Yes, it does. Presenting your ideas is a useful skill that you need to learn and practice.

S1 : Okay, I'll do my best!

123
CD2-24
2 Repeat the conversation.

124
CD2-25
3 The Students' part is missing. Listen to the conversation and speak as the Students.

125
CD2-26
4 The Teacher's part is missing. Listen to the conversation and speak as the Teacher.

5 Role play in pairs.

Check-up

■ 「…について詳しく（具体的に）説明する」は, to be specific about/in…, to elaborate on… などがある。

Elevate your knowledge

プレゼンテーションの目的は，自分の考えや情報を明確に相手に伝え，理解してもらうことです。海外留学先でも，一定のテーマに関する調査結果や意見をプレゼンテーションする課題が与えられることがあります。下記は，プレゼンテーション・スキルに関する概要です。

1 **Read the following passage and fill in the blanks with the appropriate words from the choices below.**

The two main stages in giving a presentation are preparation and ① (　　　　). Preparation consists of conducting research and organizing your ② (　　　　). You should then write up your results and reference your ③ (　　　　). Performance consists of ④ (　　　　) your speech with a clear introduction, body, and ⑤ (　　　　), and answering questions afterwards. Speed, ⑥ (　　　　), and volume are also key to a clear, effective presentation. In addition, eye contact, gestures, and ⑦ (　　　　) play an important role in making a good impression on the ⑧ (　　　　).

■選択肢■ intonation | sources | performance | conclusion | audience
posture | findings | delivering

Notes (1) プレゼンテーションでは，態度やしぐさ，また服装や表情が，言葉以上に強い印象を相手に与える場合がある。
(2) 文中の key（形容詞）は「秘訣（の）」という意味。名詞として the key to success のようにも使う。

2 **Answer the questions about the passage.**

1. What are the main stages in giving a presentation?

_____

2. What should students do after they organize their findings?

_____

3. What does a presentation performance consist of?

_____

126 02-27 3 **Listen to the passage and shadow the speaker's voice.**

127 02-28 4 **Repeat the three sentences you hear.**

Expand your vocabulary

128
CD2-29 **1** **Listen to and repeat each word. Match the English words to the Japanese words.**

1. awareness ( )   a. 環境にやさしい
2. imminent ( )   b. ラベルを貼る
3. combat ( )   c. 認識
4. label ( )   d. 放出
5. eco-friendly ( )   e. さし迫った
6. emission ( )   f. 闘う

129
CD2-30 **2** **Listen to the Japanese words and say each one in English.**

Enhance your communication skills

今日はプレゼンテーションの発表日です。マヤのトピックは「環境問題」です。多くの英語の教員も発表を聴きに来ています。

130
CD2-31 **1** **Listen to the conversation and choose the most appropriate answer.**

1. **What is the purpose of Maya's presentation?**
   a. To impress her English teachers.
   b. To help her audience to become more aware of global warming.
   c. To update her audience on the amount of CO_2 from vehicles.
   d. To promote the sale of eco-friendly products.

2. **What is the second thing she is going to talk about in her presentation?**
   a. Efforts to combat global warming.
   b. Causes of global warming.
   c. The importance of studying environmental issues.
   d. Technical difficulties in combating global warming.

3. **What is the purpose of indicating the amount of CO_2 in products?**
   a. To increase the amount of CO_2 in the atmosphere.
   b. To answer questions from the audience about CO_2.
   c. To decrease the amount of CO_2 in the atmosphere.
   d. To develop CO_2 products.

2 Listen to the conversation again and complete the sentences.

(M : Maya, T : Teacher)

M : Good afternoon, everyone. I am glad to see many of our teachers here today. Thank you for making the effort to come ①_____. Today, I'd like to talk about global warming[1]. I chose this topic because I would like to raise your awareness of this environmental issue. First, ②_____ of global warming. Second, I will outline international efforts to tackle this imminent problem. Third, I will touch upon what we can do in our daily lives to combat it. Finally, I will take any questions you might have.[2]

After the presentation

M : Well, ③_____. Does anyone have any questions?

T : Thank you for your informative presentation, Maya. My question is about labeling the amount of CO_2 on products [3]. Could you ④_____ ?

M : Of course. This kind of labeling indicates how much CO_2 has been produced before products reach consumers. Therefore, if the label includes the percent of CO_2 on it, then consumers ⑤_____. So, I think people would want to cut down on CO_2 emissions if they saw this data.

T : I agree with you. Thank you.

M : Are there any other questions? OK, then, ⑥_____.

3 Listen to the conversation and shadow the speakers' voices.

Check-up

[1] 「地球温暖化」のこと。二酸化炭素 (carbon dioxide) などの温室効果ガスによって，全世界の平均気温が上がっていく現象を指す。

[2] 「最後に，質問を受けます」という意味。プレゼンテーションの最中に質問を受ける場合は，Please feel free to interrupt me anytime if you have any questions. と言う。

[3] 温室効果ガス削減対策の一環として，いろいろな商品に二酸化炭素排出量を表示しようとする動きが高まっている。

Hosting an Online Meeting

オンライン会議

マヤは母校の留学センターから依頼され，留学予定者とのオンライン会議の司会に挑戦することにしました。

Expand your vocabulary

131 CD2-32 **1** Listen to and repeat each word. Match the English words to the Japanese words.

1.	lead	( )	a.	返答
2.	opportunity	( )	b.	登録する
3.	attend	( )	c.	（会議を）進行する
4.	sign up	( )	d.	機会
5.	collect	( )	e.	出席する
6.	response	( )	f.	集める

132 CD2-33 **2** Listen to the Japanese words and say each one in English.

Enhance your communication skills

PART 1 マヤは母校の留学カウンセラーと，オンライン会議の進め方について打ち合わせを始めました。

133 CD2-34 **1** Listen to Part 1 and circle T for true or F for false for each of the following statements.

1. Maya made a request asking her university to plan an online event.　　T / F
2. Maya has experienced hosting many online meetings.　　T / F
3. An invitation code has already been shared with participants.　　T / F

2 **Listen to Part 1 again and fill in the missing words.**

(**C** : Study Abroad Counselor, **M** : Maya)

C : Thank you for accepting our ① (　　　)(　　　)(　　　) an online
Q & A meeting [1] for students interested in studying abroad.

M : No problem. I expect to learn a lot from ②(　　　)(　　　).

C : I know you ③(　　　)(　　　) lots of online meetings.

M : Yes, but I've never been a facilitator [2] before. So, I would like to ④(　　　) a
few things with you about the online event.

C : Sure. ⑤(　　　)(　　　) the schedule for that day.

M : The ⑥(　　　) of this event is to answer questions about study abroad life
from next year's students, right?

C : Yes. Eleven people ⑦(　　　)(　　　)(　　　) so far. I've already
sent the ⑧(　　　)(　　　) to them.

M : I'm ⑨(　　　) to talk with them. Plus, I want to invite some of my friends to
join the online event, as well. Is that okay?

C : Great. The more information that the students can get, ⑩(　　　)
(　　　).

3 **Repeat the conversation.**

4 **Maya's part is missing. Listen to the conversation and speak as Maya.**

5 **The Study Abroad Counselor's part is missing. Listen to the conversation
and speak as the Study Abroad Counselor.**

6 **Role play in pairs.**

Check-up

[1] 「online meeting」は web meeting や remote meeting ということもある。関連用語として「オンラインセミナー」を webinar (web + seminar) という。

[2] 会議などの「進行役・まとめ役」という意味。

1 **Put the words in parentheses in the correct order.**

C : How many of your friends will be joining?

M : Two. Each of them is going to access the video conference system from home.

C : Alright. Could you share your friends' e-mail addresses with me?

M : Yes, I'll do that later today. And can I make another suggestion? ① (don't / advance / collect / some / why / questions / in / we)?

C : That's a great idea, and that ② (you / help / give / will / answers / well-prepared) to the students.

M : On the day of the event, we'll show the list of questions first, along with our responses. Does that sound okay to you?

C : Yes. In an online meeting, we often ③ (run / end / out / time / at / of / the). This way, we'll have enough time to answer additional questions from students.

136
CD 2-37 **2** **Repeat the conversation.**

137
CD 2-38 **3** **Maya's part is missing. Listen to the conversation and speak as Maya.**

138
CD 2-39 **4** **The Study Abroad Counselor's part is missing. Listen to the conversation and speak as the Study Abroad Counselor.**

5 **Role play in pairs.**

Elevate your knowledge

昨今はオンラインで授業に参加したり配信講義を受講することが当たり前になってきました。下記は，オンライン会議で役立つ留意点です。

1 **Read the following passage and fill in the blanks with the appropriate words from the choices below.**

Recent video conference platforms allow users to communicate ① (　　　　) with a small amount of ② (　　　　), such as a tablet or laptop computer with a headset. Remote accessibility is one of the advantages of online meetings over traditional face-to-face meetings. Here are some ③ (　　　　) for making online meetings more effective. When it is your turn to talk, speak clearly and ④ (　　　　). As background noises can ⑤ (　　　　) others, mute the microphone except when you are talking. In addition, too much information ⑥ (　　　　) onto one slide makes the audience tired, so create simple and easy-to-see ⑦ (　　　　) materials. Finally, ask participants to write their comments and questions in the chat box during your meeting. This allows you to ⑧ (　　　　) with information that needs clarification.

選択肢 crammed | virtually | concisely | equipment | visual | tips |
distract | respond

Notes video conference platform の他にも online conference system や online meeting software などの呼び方があり，教育現場で仮想教室 virtual classroom やオンデマンド講義 on-demand lecture に使われる。

2 **Answer the questions about the passage.**

1. What tools do users need for virtual communication today?

   _____

2. How can participants avoid background noises in an online meeting?

   _____

3. Why are simple and easy-to-see materials preferable?

   _____

139
2-40
3 **Listen to the passage and shadow the speaker's voice.**

140
2-41
4 **Repeat the three sentences you hear.**

Expand your vocabulary

1 **Listen to and repeat each word. Match the English words to the Japanese words.**

1. thrilled   ( )   a. 会合
2. facilitate   ( )   b. わくわくしている
3. session   ( )   c. 心配
4. concern   ( )   d. 機能
5. microphone   ( )   e. 司会進行する
6. function   ( )   f. マイク

2 **Listen to the Japanese words and say each one in English.**

Enhance your communication skills

マヤが進行役のオンライン会議が始まりました。オンライン会議ならではの確認事項もあるようです。

1 **Listen to the conversation and choose the most appropriate answer.**

1. **What is the purpose of the online event that Maya will facilitate?**
   a. To invite students to a new study abroad program in Japan.
   b. To help students feel less anxious about going on a study abroad program.
   c. To introduce her friends to new international students.
   d. To teach students how to use a video conference system.

2. **After the session starts, what will be done first?**
   a. Facilitators will send a greeting message to the chat box.
   b. Participants will have time to introduce themselves.
   c. Questions will be gathered from the participants.
   d. Answers to the questions will be displayed to the participants.

3. **Which is NOT mentioned as a way for a participant to communicate with the facilitators?**
   a. Through an e-mail account
   b. In the chat box function
   c. With a microphone
   d. Using a reaction icon

143
2-44

2 Listen to the conversation again and complete the sentences.

(M : Maya,　F2 : Facilitator 2,　F3 : Facilitator 3)

M : Good morning, everyone. Can you hear me clearly? Thank you for attending today's online Q & A meeting. I'm thrilled to join you today. My name is Maya and ① _____ today's session with two friends who have studied abroad.

Maya's two friends take turns introducing themselves.

F2 : Before we start, let me share a few things about today's online meeting. First, the main purpose of today's session is to answer your questions about study abroad life. We hope this discussion ② _____. So, we're going to show our responses to your questions ③ _____ this session.

F3 : Next, you might have new questions during the session. You can use the chat box function or speak through the microphone[1] ④ _____ _____ your questions and comments. If you click on the raise hand icon[2], we'll say your name so you can talk. ⑤ _____ ? Now, let's start our discussion.

At the end of the Q & A session

M : We got a lot done today. Thank you for your participation, everyone. ⑥ _____ and have a great study abroad experience. See you soon here in San Francisco!

143
2-44

3 Listen to the conversation and shadow the speakers' voices.

Check-up

[1] mic や mike と略すこともある。
[2] ビデオ会議ツールで参加者が挙手していることを伝えるために押す「挙手ボタン」のこと。raise hand button ともいう。「反応ボタン」reaction button の一種で，他に「いいね・賛成」thumbs up, 「拍手」clap などさまざまな種類がある。

Encountering New Food Habits

新しい食文化

留学先では，日本とは異なるさまざまな食文化に触れる機会が増えます。マヤも新しい発見をしたようです。

1

Expand your vocabulary

144
CD 2-45
1 Listen to and repeat each word. Match the English words to the Japanese words.

1. farewell ( ) a. 禁止する
2. potluck party ( ) b. （料理の）材料
3. beverage ( ) c. 送別の
4. prohibit ( ) d. 飲料
5. certify ( ) e. 持ち寄りパーティー
6. ingredient ( ) f. 認証する

145
CD 2-46
2 Listen to the Japanese words and say each one in English.

Enhance your communication skills

PART 1 マヤは，ベトナムからの留学生ビェンと話しています。ビェンは送別会を企画しています。

146
CD 2-47
1 Listen to Part 1 and circle T for true or F for false for each of the following statements.

1. Maya is going to participate in a farewell party next week. T / F
2. The party guests are asked to bring food and drinks. T / F
3. One guest is unable to drink alcohol because of his/her allergy. T / F

2 Listen to Part 1 again and fill in the missing words.

(B : Bien, M : Maya)

B : Hi Maya, I'm planning to hold a ①(　　　　)(　　　　) next week. It's a
②(　　　　) event for one of my housemates. It would be great to have you
there, too.

M : Thanks so much for the invitation. ③(　　　　)(　　　　)(　　　　)!

B : Wonderful, I'll send you the location by text. It's a ④(　　　　)(　　　　).
So, please bring something that you think everyone will enjoy eating or drinking.

M : Okay, I'll bring something special to ⑤(　　　　)(　　　　) everyone.

B : Thank you, but I have one request. Please ⑥(　　　　)(　　　　) alcoholic
beverages[1].

M : Oh, ⑦(　　　　)(　　　　) curiosity, why is that?

B : The housemate that is leaving is a Muslim[2]. He ⑧(　　　　)(　　　　)
alcohol. Alcohol is an example of a ⑨(　　　　) beverage for Muslims.

M : ⑩(　　　　)(　　　　). Then I'll buy soft drinks instead.

3 Repeat the conversation.

4 Maya's part is missing. Listen to the conversation and speak as Maya.

5 Bien's part is missing. Listen to the conversation and speak as Bien.

6 Role play in pairs.

Check·up

■ 「お酒」という意味でアルコール飲料を総称するときに使う。単に alcohol ということもある。日常会話では have a drink 「(お酒を) 一杯飲む」のように drink を使うことも多い。

■ 「イスラム教徒・イスラム教を信仰する人」の意味。Buddhist 「仏教徒」, Christian 「キリスト教徒」と同様に頭文字は大文字で書く。「イスラム教」は Islam と表し, 形容詞は Islamic。

PART 2 ビェンが，イスラム教の食事制限についてマヤに説明しています。

1 **Put the words in parentheses in the correct order.**

M : Are there any foods that Muslims don't eat?

B : Yes, there are some foods, such as pork ❸, which are not allowed.

M : I didn't know that. How ① (foods / you / which / do / or / know) drinks are allowed?

B : Many foods and drinks have a halal sign on the package.

M : Halal signs? What are they?

B : ② (on / they / symbols / printed /are) food and drink packages. They show where the item is produced and certify that it is ③ (prohibited / any / ingredients / of / free).

M : So, I can easily recognize which products Muslims can eat or drink.

B : That's right.

2 **Repeat the conversation.**

3 **Maya's part is missing. Listen to the conversation and speak as Maya.**

4 **Bien's part is missing. Listen to the conversation and speak as Bien.**

5 **Role play in pairs.**

Check·up

❸ 「豚肉」のこと。「牛肉」は beef，「鶏肉（ニワトリの肉）」は chicken。他にもさまざまな種類の食肉があるが，豚肉・牛肉に限らず「動物の肉」を meat，ニワトリに限らず「鳥の肉」を poultry と総称し，スーパーマーケットの「精肉コーナー」は meat(s) and poultry という。

Elevate your knowledge

他の国からの留学生とランチタイムを過ごしたり，レストランに行くことは留学生活でしかできない経験のひとつです。下記は，知っておくとよいさまざまな食文化の概要です。

1 **Read the following passage and fill in the blanks with the appropriate words from the choices below.**

International students often ①(   ) food habits that are new for them. Halal foods and Kosher foods are the most common ②(   ) foods from Islam and Judaism, respectively, which include restrictions. In some cases, food habits ③(   ) people's lifestyles. Vegetarians have ④(   ) to a growing number of restaurants offering non-meat options. Also, drinking restrictions ⑤(   ) by country, state, or even ⑥(   ). Young international students must be particularly ⑦(   ) of the local laws ⑧(   ) under-age drinking because these rules may be quite different from what is allowed in their home countries.

■選択肢■ region | vary | encounter | contributed | reflect | aware | religious | against

Notes (1)respectively は「それぞれ」という意味。Hanako and Taro are 10 and 12 years old, respectively. のように，通例文尾に置いて情報が述べられた順に対になっていることを示す。
(2) 公共の場での飲酒を厳しく制限している国や地域もあり，歩道や路面のカフェ・公園で飲酒すると留学生や観光客でも軽犯罪として処分をうける可能性がある。

2 **Answer the questions about the passage.**

1. What two religious foods with restrictions are mentioned?

_____

2. Vegetarians have a different food habit than other people, what is it?

_____

3. What should young international students be careful to know in each country?

_____

 3 **Listen to the passage and shadow the speaker's voice.**

 4 **Repeat the three sentences you hear.**

Expand your vocabulary

1 **Listen to and repeat each word. Match the English words to the Japanese words.**

1. order ( ) a. 〜を表す
2. dish ( ) b. 身分証明（書）
3. stand for ( ) c. 注文する
4. serve ( ) d. 確認
5. identification ( ) e. 料理
6. verification ( ) f. 食事を出す

2 **Listen to the Japanese words and say each one in English.**

Enhance your communication skills

マヤの友人タケルは初めてのレストランで注文しています。

1 **Listen to the conversation and choose the most appropriate answer.**

1. **What will Takeru have today?**
   a. A vegan curry & soup combo with a local beer.
   b. A non-vegan curry & soup combo with a local beer.
   c. A vegan curry & soup combo without a local beer.
   d. A non-vegan curry & soup combo without a local beer.

2. **Which is true about the restaurant?**
   a. It is a self-service style restaurant.
   b. Every dish on its menu has a vegan option.
   c. They serve a wide range of beer.
   d. It does not accept under-aged students as guests.

3. **What problem does Takeru have at the restaurant?**
   a. He has not reached the legal drinking age.
   b. He cannot prove his age.
   c. He must drive back home after drinking.
   d. He is allergic to local beer.

2 Listen to the conversation again and complete the sentences.

(R : Restaurant Wait Staff, T : Takeru)

R : Are you ready to order?

T : I'll have the chef's curry & soup combo. By the way, there is a symbol next to the dish name. ①_____?

R : The symbol shows that a vegan **1** option ②_____. Dishes with this mark can be served as vegan ③_____.

T : Thanks for telling me. ④_____ the vegan option today.

R : All right. Will that be all?

T : Well, what local beers do you have?

R : ⑤_____, but you look a little young. The legal drinking age **2** is 21 in California.

T : I turned 21 last month. **3**

R : Do you have any identification **4** to show your age, please?

T : Oh, I didn't bring my passport with me today.

R : I'm sorry, but we can't serve alcohol ⑥_____.

T : Is my student ID okay?

R : Unfortunately, no. The chai tea is a popular choice. Would you like to order that?

T : Yes, that sounds good.

3 Listen to the conversation and shadow the speakers' voices.

Check·up

1 「完全菜食主義」またはそのような食生活をする人のこと。菜食主義 vegetarian との違いは、動物性の食品を避ける食生活を徹底する点といわれる（※ Extra Exercise も参照）。

2 「法定飲酒年齢」のこと。LDA と省略されることもある。

3 「先月 21 歳になった」という意味。「〜歳になる」は become ではなく turn で表す。

4 海外ではパスポートがもっとも公的で確実な身分証となるが，紛失や盗難のおそれがあるので携帯にはくれぐれも注意が必要である。

Shopping

買い物

マヤは町で買い物を楽しんでいます。

Expand your vocabulary

157 **CD 2-58** **1** Listen to and repeat each word. Match the English words to the Japanese words.

1. sold out ( ) a. 〜を申し込む
2. excluding ( ) b. 受けつける
3. gift-wrap ( ) c. 売り切れの
4. accept ( ) d. 購入品
5. apply for ( ) e. 〜を除いて
6. purchase ( ) f. 贈り物用に包む

158 **CD 2-59** **2** Listen to the Japanese words and say each one in English.

Enhance your communication skills

PART 1　マヤは町の免税店に入って買い物をすることにしました。マヤと店員の会話です。

159 **CD 2-60** **1** Listen to Part 1 and circle T for true or F for false for each of the following statements.

1. Maya is buying a present for her sister.　　　　　　　　　　T / F
2. Maya chooses to buy a white item.　　　　　　　　　　　　T / F
3. The item Maya is buying costs $75.60.　　　　　　　　　　T / F

2 Listen to Part 1 again and fill in the missing words.

(C : Clerk, M : Maya)

C : Hello, have you been ① (　　　　　　) yet? **1**

M : No, not yet. Could I have a look at the white bag on that ② (　　　　　), please?

C : ③ (　　　　　). It's a new ④ (　　　　　). We just got it last week.

M : Oh, really? Hmmm... This design looks good and feels soft.

C : That's a new style this season. Is this bag for yourself or a present for someone?

M : I'm looking for a bag for my mother. I wonder if you have a smaller one of the same kind and color.

C : Just a moment, please. Well, this one is the same ⑤ (　　　　　) in the smaller size, but it's ⑥ (　　　　　). The smaller white one is sold out.

M : Oh, I see. Actually, I like this beige one better and the size is perfect. What's the price? **2**

C : It's ⑦ (　　　　　) excluding tax.

M : Hmm... OK, I'll take it. Can you ⑧ (　　　　　) it, please?

C : Certainly. How would you like to pay for this?

M : Do you accept ⑨ (　　　　)(　　　　) ? **3**

C : Sure. Or would you be interested in applying for an ⑩ (　　　　　) credit card?

M : Oh, no, thank you.

C : Okay. Please wait while the customer service clerk wraps your purchase.

M : Thank you.

3 Repeat the conversation.

4 Maya's part is missing. Listen to the conversation and speak as Maya.

5 The Clerk's part is missing. Listen to the conversation and speak as the Clerk.

6 Role play in pairs.

Check·up

1 「ご用を伺っていますか」という店員の決まり文句。何も買う気がないときは I'm just window-shopping. または I'm just looking. などと言う。

2 値段を聞く表現として，How much is it? / How much does it cost? などもある。

3 「クレジットカードで支払えますか」という意味。現金で支払うときは，I'd like to pay in cash. と言う。

1 **Put the words in parentheses in the correct order.**

C : OK, you're all set. You can pick up your purchase at ① (counter / the / Customer / in / Service / ten) minutes.

M : Oh. ② (up / I / it / here / don't / pick)?

C : No, I'm sorry. Our department store ③ (special / gift / has / for / counter / a / wrapping).

M : Oh, I see. Thanks for your help.

C : You're welcome. Have a nice day.

M : You too.

162 CD2-63   **2** **Repeat the conversation.**

163 CD2-64   **3** **Maya's part is missing. Listen to the conversation and speak as Maya.**

164 CD2-65   **4** **The Clerk's part is missing. Listen to the conversation and speak as the Clerk.**

5 **Role play in pairs.**

Elevate your knowledge

海外での買い物は楽しみのひとつであり，現地の生活を肌で感じる良い機会でもあります。下記は，海外での買い物と通貨の携行方法についてです。

1 Read the following passage and fill in the blanks with the appropriate words from the choices below.

Visiting local shops or stores can ①(　　　　　　) students with the opportunity to ②(　　　　　　) with the everyday lives of local people. However, for ③(　　　　　　) reasons, students are advised not to carry large amounts of ④(　　　　　　) when shopping overseas. Therefore, it is advisable to apply for a ⑤(　　　　　　) that has no fees for international purchases before leaving Japan. Also, they can easily ⑥(　　　　　　) if lost or stolen. Recent ⑦(　　　　　　) indicate that more Japanese students use credit cards because of the ⑧(　　　　　　) when shopping overseas and also to earn reward points.

■選択肢■ be replaced | cash | provide | convenience | become familiar | credit card | trends | security

Notes credit card は VISA, Master Card などの国際カードであれば日本国内と同様に使える。

2 Answer the questions about the passage.

1. In what way is visiting local shops or stores good for students?

   _____

2. What are students advised not to do when shopping overseas?

   _____

3. What is the best way for students to purchase something while shopping overseas?

   _____

165
02-66 **3** Listen to the passage and shadow the speaker's voice.

166
02-67 **4** Repeat the three sentences you hear.

Expand your vocabulary

 1 **Listen to and repeat each word. Match the English words to the Japanese words.**

1.	round-neck	( )	a.	疑う
2.	fitting room	( )	b.	手作りの
3.	doubt	( )	c.	高価な
4.	key chain	( )	d.	試着室
5.	handmade	( )	e.	丸首の
6.	pricey	( )	f.	キーホルダー

2 **Listen to the Japanese words and say each one in English.**

Enhance your communication skills

マヤは，夕方出かけるときに着る衣類を買いに店に来ています。

 1 **Listen to the conversation and choose the most appropriate answer.**

1. **What does Maya want to buy?**
   a. She wants a blue or a red blouse.
   b. She wants a red or a green sweater.
   c. She wants a red v-neck sweater.
   d. She wants a round-neck sweater.

2. **What seems to be the problem?**
   a. There are no red sweaters in size 10.
   b. There are no sweaters in Maya's size.
   c. There is a sweater in Maya's size, but it's green.
   d. All the red sweaters are sold out.

3. **Why doesn't Maya buy a key chain?**
   a. She can't find any good key chains.
   b. The key chains are too expensive.
   c. She doesn't like the color.
   d. She is not fond of leather key chains.

2 Listen to the conversation again and complete the sentences.

(**M** : Maya, **C** : Clerk)

M : Excuse me. What are these round-neck sweaters ①_____?

C : They are made of wool ■ and cotton.

M : ②_____?

C : Of course. What color do you like?

M : Do you have it in blue or red?

C : Yes, we have both colors. However, I think red might suit you better than blue. Why don't you try it in red?

M : All right. What size do you think I need?

C : Maybe around size 8. You can use that fitting room over there... ③_____?

M : Well, it's a little loose and the sleeves are a bit too long. Do you have it ④_____?

C : Maybe, I'll check. Well, I have a smaller size, but in a different color. We only have one size 6 left and it's green. Would you like to try it on?

M : Yes, please... Well, this fits me much better. But I'm sorry, I don't like the color very much. Will you be getting more red ones in soon?

C : So sorry, but I doubt it. However, let me check our other store.

After checking

C : Good news. Union Square store has a red sweater in size 6. Would you like to have them put it on hold for you?

M : Yes, that'd be great. I'll go there later today. By the way, I'm interested in those brown key chains in the show case.

C : They're handmade of real leather.

M : Really? How much are they?

C : They are all ⑤_____.

M : Oh, they're pricier than I thought. ⑥_____. Thank you, anyway.

C : Thank you. Have a nice day!

M : You too.

3 Listen to the conversation and shadow the speakers' voices.

Check-up

■ 「羊毛」のこと。「綿」は cotton,「麻」は linen,「絹」は silk,「カシミヤ」は cashmere,「合成繊維」は synthetic fibers,「ポリエステル」は polyester。

Airport Departure Procedures

出国手続き

マヤたちは 5 週間の研修を終え，帰国することになりました。

Expand your vocabulary

170
CD 2-71

1. Listen to and repeat each word. Match the English words to the Japanese words.

1.	cabin	( )	a.	手荷物
2.	suit	( )	b.	確認する
3.	luggage	( )	c.	楽しい
4.	scale	( )	d.	はかり
5.	confirm	( )	e.	適する
6.	pleasant	( )	f.	（航空機の）客室

171
CD 2-72

2. Listen to the Japanese words and say each one in English.

Enhance your communication skills

PART 1　マヤは空港の航空会社のチェックイン・カウンター前に並び，搭乗手続きの順番を待っています。

172
CD 2-73

1. Listen to Part 1 and circle T for true or F for false for each of the following statements.

1. Maya would like a seat in the front of the plane.   T / F
2. Maya's seat is in the back of the plane.   T / F
3. Maya wants to bring two bags on board.   T / F

2 **Listen to Part 1 again and fill in the missing words.**

(C : Clerk, M : Maya)

C : May I help the next person ①(   )(   )∎, please?

M : Hello. I'd like to ②(   )(   )(   ) the flight to Tokyo, please.

C : Certainly. May I see your reservation and passport, please?

M : Yes, here you are.

C : Thanks.

M : Is it possible to change my seat to one in the front of the ③(   ), please?

C : Well, today's flight is ④(   )(   ), but let me see what I can do.

M : Thanks. I'd ⑤(   ) it.

C : Sorry, but we have no seats left near the front. We do have a window seat in the ⑥(   ) of the plane. Does that suit you?

M : Yes, it does. Thanks.

C : Alright, your new seat is 30A. How many pieces of ⑦(   ) will you be checking in?

M : I have two suitcases and this bag. I would like to take this one ⑧(   ) (   ) with me.

C : That's fine. That small bag will fit under your seat. Could you place your suitcase on the scale for me, please?

M : Sure. Here you go.

C : Now, here's your ⑨(   )(   ), ⑩(   )(   ) (   ), and your passport. You're all set. Please go through the security check at least 45 minutes before your flight.

M : Thanks so much for your help.

C : Have a good flight to Tokyo.

3 **Repeat the conversation.**

4 **Maya's part is missing. Listen to the conversation and speak as Maya.**

5 **The Clerk's part is missing. Listen to the conversation and speak as the Clerk.**

6 **Role play in pairs.**

Check·up

∎ 「順番を待つ列」をアメリカでは line, イギリス英語圏では queue と呼ぶ。

1　**Put the words in parentheses in the correct order.**

C : Your boarding time is 10:30 at Gate E34. Please make sure that ① (at / before / the / you're / least / at / gate / 20 minutes / boarding).

M : OK. By the way, could you confirm if my friend, Yuka Tanaka ② (checked / for / has / this / in / already / flight)?

C : Sorry, I am not allowed to share that information with you.

M : Oh, I see. No, problem. Thank you anyway.

C : You're welcome. ③ (flight / a / have / pleasant).

2 **Repeat the conversation.**

3 **Maya's part is missing. Listen to the conversation and speak as Maya.**

4 **The Clerk's part is missing. Listen to the conversation and speak as the Clerk.**

5 **Role play in pairs.**

Elevate your knowledge

出国の手続きには，航空会社のチェックイン・カウンターでの搭乗手続きと，手荷物検査や出国審査などがあります。そのあと，ゲートへと移動します。下記は，空港での出国手続きの概要です。

1 Read the following passage and fill in the blanks with the appropriate words from the choices below.

For international flights, passengers are advised to ①(　　　　　) at least two hours ②(　　　　　) departure. They must first go to the check-in counter and show their flight reservation and passports. At that time, they can ③(　　　　　) to change their seats and then check in all ④(　　　　　) except for ⑤(　　　　　) bags. They then receive a ⑥(　　　　　) and baggage claim tags. After that, they should ⑦(　　　　　) the security check and go through ⑧(　　　　　) before going to their gate. If time allows, there are duty-free shops and restaurants inside the terminal that can be enjoyed before take-off.

選択肢 luggage | request | check in | prior to | carry-on | boarding pass | proceed to | immigration

Notes (1)「携帯手荷物」は，carry-on bag, carry-on/cabin/hand baggage と呼ぶ。
(2)「搭乗券」を boarding pass と呼び，座席 (seat)，搭乗口 (gate)，行先 (destination)，便名 (flight)，出発時間 (departure time) などが記載されている。
(3)「委託手荷物」を checked luggage と言い，航空会社の名札 (tag) が付けられ，その半券（claim tag）を受け取る。

2 Answer the questions about the passage.

1.　When are passengers advised to check in?

_____

2.　What do passengers have to show in order to check in?

_____

3.　What is the term for luggage that is taken on board?

_____

 3 Listen to the passage and shadow the speaker's voice.

4 Repeat the three sentences you hear.

Expand your vocabulary

 1 **Listen to and repeat each word. Match the English words to the Japanese words.**

1. backpack ( )   a. 機内持ち込み手荷物
2. carry-on ( )   b. 重量制限
3. weight limit ( )   c. バックパック（リュックサック）
4. surcharge ( )   d. 物
5. stuff ( )   e. 捨てる
6. throw away ( )   f. 超過料金

 2 **Listen to the Japanese words and say each one in English.**

Enhance your communication skills

マヤの友人のユカは，マヤより遅れて空港に着き，搭乗手続きをしようとしています。

1 **Listen to the conversation and choose the most appropriate answer.**

1. **What is the problem with Yuka's suitcase?**
   a. It's too small.
   b. It's too large.
   c. It's too expensive.
   d. It's too heavy.

2. **What did Yuka do when she was told to pay the surcharge?**
   a. She paid it without hesitation.
   b. She took out some stuff from her suitcase and put it in her backpack.
   c. She threw away some stuff that she didn't need.
   d. She borrowed money from her friend.

3. **How will she get to the boarding gate from the check-in counter?**
   a. She will turn right and go down the escalator after passing through security.
   b. She will turn right and go upstairs after passing through security.
   c. She will make a left and take the elevator before passing through security.
   d. She will make a right and go up the escalator before passing through security.

2 Listen to the conversation again and complete the sentences.

(Y : Yuka, C : Clerk)

Y : Good morning. ① _____ the flight to Tokyo?

C : Yes. May I have your reservation information and your passport?

Y : Sure. Here you go.

C : Thank you. Would you put your suitcase here, please? Do you have any other luggage?

Y : Yes, I have this backpack. I would like to ② _____ .

C : That's fine. Oh, I'm afraid your suitcase is over ■ the weight limit.

Y : Sorry? What did you say?

C : Your suitcase is too heavy. I'm sorry, but you'll have to pay a surcharge of $120.

Y : Oh no! I don't have that much money on me. What should I do?

C : Well, maybe③ _____ from your suitcase and put it in your backpack. Also if there is anything you don't need, you can throw it away in the trash bins in the waiting area.

Y : I see. I will take my books out. OK, ④ _____ . How is the suitcase now?

C : Let's see. It's okay, now.

Y : Oh, good!

C : Now, where would you like to sit? An aisle seat or a window seat?

Y : ⑤ _____ , please.

C : All right. Your seat number is 37C. Here is your boarding pass, passport and luggage claim tag.

Y : Thank you for your help.

C : Sure. Your boarding time is 10:30 at gate E34. Make a right and go up the escalator ⑥ _____ .

Y : Thank you again.

C : You're welcome. Have a nice flight.

3 Listen to the conversation and shadow the speakers' voices.

Check-up

■ 「…を越える」という意味では, exceed..., surpass... なども使える。

Keeping in Touch

eメール

日本に帰国したマヤは，アメリカでのホームステイ先や友人に e メールを送ります。

Expand your vocabulary

183
CD2-84
1 Listen to and repeat each word. Match the English words to the Japanese words.

1. hospitality ( ) a. 添付する
2. treat ( ) b. 答える
3. respond ( ) c. 奨学金
4. scholarship ( ) d. 入学
5. admission ( ) e. 歓待
6. attach ( ) f. もてなす

184
CD2-85
2 Listen to the Japanese words and say each one in English.

Enhance your communication skills

PART 1　日本に帰国したマヤからホームステイ先のケイとジャックに宛てた e メールです。

185
CD2-86
1 Listen to Part 1 and circle T for true or F for false for each of the following statements.

1. Kay and Jack took good care of Maya while she was with them.　　T / F
2. Maya upset Kay and Jack by asking questions at dinner time.　　T / F
3. Maya has decided not to study abroad at an American university in the future.

T / F

2 **Listen to Part 1 again and fill in the missing words.**

From: "Maya Asada" maya24@xxxxxx.ne.jp

Date：March 30, 20xx

To: "The Fenton Family" fenton@xxxxxxxx.com

Subject：Greetings from Maya

Dear Kay and Jack,

How are things with you? I hope both of you are well. I am writing to **1**
①(   ) my deep ②(   ) for your hospitality during my stay with you.
I am especially ③(   )(   ) you for ④(   ) me like a member
of your family.

I ⑤(   ) the wonderful times we shared together. ⑥(   ) over dinner
with you allowed me the chance to ⑦(   )(   ) English, and to learn
about the U.S. and life in San Francisco. I hope I did not bother you too much with my
silly questions. You always responded kindly to my questions with clear and interesting
answers.

Because of my experience in America, I am very interested in studying at an overseas
university in the future. I will ⑧(   )(   ) study abroad options
being offered to international students. Also, I will check out what scholarships are
⑨(   )(   ) me at my university. In any case, I have to get a
⑩(   )(   ) on TOEFL **2** for admission to university. But I'll do my
best to make my dreams come true.

3 **Repeat the text.**

Check-up
1 「～するために書いております」という類似表現には，This is to... がある。
2 Test of English as Foreign Language の略である。アメリカなどの大学は，英語を母国語と
しない入学申請者に対して TOEFL や IELTS のスコアの提出を要求している。

PART 2 マヤはケイとジャックへの e メールを締めくくります。

1 Put the words in parentheses in the correct order.

① (coming / if / feel / you / ever / like) to Japan, you are most welcome to stay with my family in Kyoto. You can visit the places that I described to you while I was in the U.S, such as Fushimi Inari Shrine or Nijō Castle. Also, my friend Yuka who came to the potluck party at your home asked me to ② (regards / to / you / her/ give) **4** . ③ (seeing / I / looking / again / to / am / you / forward). Let's keep in touch and talk often.

Miss you, **5**

Maya

P.S. **6** I attached three photos of us together to this e-mail. I hope you like them.

2 Repeat the text.

Check·up

- **4** 「…によろしくお伝えください」の意味で，send/convey... my regards, say hello to... for me とも言える。
- **5** 親しい人への手紙やメールで使われる結びのことば。
- **6** postscript の略で，「追伸」のことである。

Elevate your knowledge

技術や通信環境の進展により、日々のやり取りはパソコンの e メールや携帯電話のアプリを使って行われるようになりました。下記は、それらのコミュニケーション手段についての説明です。

1 **Read the following passage and fill in the blanks with the appropriate words from the choices below.**

Communication through ①(   ) includes using smartphone apps, such as LINE or WhatsApp, to stay in ②(   ) with new friends or ③(   ). Tech-savvy students [(1)] use social media platforms to send direct messages (DM), forward YouTube links, and ④(   ) photos on a regular basis. Today's students become ⑤(   ) as they share video clips and photos on Instagram and TikTok. Another communication tool is e-mail. The use of e-mail, which is short for [(2)] electronic mail, is also used for business or ⑥(   ) purposes. Features [(3)] of smartphone apps and e-mail include their high speed, low cost, and large ⑦(   ). Furthermore, it is possible to share information with ⑧(   ) people simultaneously.

選択肢 storage capacity | post | acquaintances | multiple | social media | academic | touch | influencers

Notes (1) Tech-savvy students は Technology-savvy students でテクノロジーに精通した学生のこと。
(2)...is short for... は「…は…の省略形である」という意味。
(3) feature は「特徴」で，同意語としては characteristic, trait, attribute などがある。

2 **Answer the questions about the passage.**

1. What is LINE or WhatsApp used for?

_____

2. What do tech-savvy students do through social media sites?

_____

3. What are some common features of smartphone apps and e-mail?

_____

187
2-88 3 **Listen to the passage and shadow the speaker's voice.**

188
2-89 4 **Repeat the three sentences you hear.**

Expand your vocabulary

189
CD 2-90

1 **Listen to and repeat each word. Match the English words to the Japanese words.**

1. fond ( ) a. 観光産業
2. intriguing ( ) b. 懐かしい
3. graduate school ( ) c. 通訳
4. tourism ( ) d. 大学院
5. interpretation ( ) e. さしあたり
6. in the meantime ( ) f. 興味をそそる

190
CD 2-91

2 **Listen to the Japanese words and say each one in English.**

Enhance your communication skills

マヤは，帰国後，アメリカで知り合ったスーに宛ててeメールを書きました。

191
CD 2-92

1 **Listen to the text and choose the most appropriate answer.**

1. **Where was Sue two months ago?**
   a. In Japan.
   b. In Australia.
   c. In Taiwan.
   d. In America.

2. **How did Maya feel about giving presentations in class?**
   a. She found it boring but rewarding.
   b. She found it tough but rewarding.
   c. She found it intriguing but easy.
   d. She found it easy but boring.

3. **What was Sue planning to do?**
   a. She was planning to meet Maya in Japan.
   b. She was planning to study at an institution of higher education overseas.
   c. She was planning to study tourism and hospitality in Taiwan.
   d. She was planning to give Maya advice for studying in America.

2 **Listen to the text again and complete the sentences.**

From："Maya Asada" maya24@xxxxxx.ne.jp

Date：May 20, 20xx

To："Sue Chan" suechan@xxxxxxxxl.com

Subject：Hello from Japan

Dear Sue,

Hello! Wow, I can't believe it's been almost two months since I returned to Japan from America. ①＿＿＿＿＿＿＿＿＿＿＿＿＿＿＿＿! I guess you are back in Taiwan by now. When I think about my classes in the States**1**, I know that I was very lucky to have you as one of my classmates.②＿＿＿＿＿＿＿＿＿＿＿＿ we had together in class and after school. I miss you and the good times we had in Fisherman's Wharf with our friends.

Joining the English program at San Francisco Griffith University was my first time to ③＿＿＿＿＿＿＿＿＿＿＿＿＿ with students of different nationalities. I was amazed at how outgoing you were and how friendly many others in class were, too. I found activities in class, such as giving presentations, very intriguing but challenging. However, even though it was hard, it was rewarding and ④＿＿＿＿＿＿＿＿＿＿ ＿＿＿ and important global issues.

You told me you were planning to go to graduate school in Australia or America. How is that plan coming along? I am interested in studying either tourism or interpretation at an institution of higher education in Australia or America, too. Do you have any advice ⑤＿＿＿＿＿＿＿＿＿＿＿＿?

I hope to see you again sometime in the near future. In the meantime, please take good care of yourself.

⑥＿＿＿＿＿＿＿＿＿＿＿＿＿.

All the best,

Maya

3 **Listen to the text and shadow the speaker's voice.**

Check-up

1 in the States は「アメリカで（の）」。down under は「オーストラリアで（の）／ニュージーランドで（の）」。

Extra Exercises

Chapter 1

Exercise 1

下は, 留学の **Application Form**（応募様式）の一例です。各項目はそれぞれどういう意味でしょうか。（　　）に日本語の意味を書きましょう。

Exercise 2

下の **Application Form** に自分の情報を書きいれてみましょう。

Personal Information		
Last Name / Surname (　　　　　　　　　　)	First Name / Given Name (　　　　　　　　　　)	Middle Name [if applicable] (　　　　　　　　　　)
Date of Birth [mm/dd/yyyy] (　　　　　　　　　　)	Gender (　　　　　　　　　　)	Country of Citizenship (　　　　　　　　　　)
	☐ Male ☐ Female ☐ X (　　　　　　　　　　)	
Passport Number (　　　　　　　　　　)	Passport Expiration Date (　　　　　　　　　　)	

Contact Information		
Address (　　　　　　　　　　)		
Postal Code (　　　　　　　　　　)	Phone Number [Home] (　　　　　　　　　　)	Phone Number [Mobile] (　　　　　　　　　　)

Program Information

Course Name ( )	Reason for Application ( )
Length of Study ( )	
Residence Type ( )	
☐ Dormitory ( ) ☐ Homestay ( ) ☐ Apartment ( )	

Academic Information

Name of College / University Currently Attending ( )		Current Year ( )
		☐ 1st ☐ 2nd ☐ 3rd ☐ 4th
Name of Department [Major] ( )		Expected Year of Graduation ( )
Average Grade [Current GPA] ( )	English Proficiency Level ( )	English Language Certification ( )
☐ 3.5-4.0 ☐ 3.0-3.4 ☐ 2.5-2.9 ☐ 2.4 and below	☐ Beginner ( ) ☐ Lower Intermediate ( ) ☐ Upper Intermediate ( ) ☐ Advanced ( )	☐ TOEIC ☐ TOEFL ☐ IELTS ☐ CAMBRIDGE

Chapter

Exercise 1

機内の英語表示です。それぞれどういう意味でしょうか。空欄を埋めましょう。

Signs located in the cabin	機内の表示
FASTEN SEAT BELT	
RETURN TO SEAT	

Signs in the rest room	トイレの表示
OCCUPIED	
VACANT	
FLUSH	
LOCK	
UNLOCK	
NO SMOKING	

Exercise 2

次は機内アナウンスです。それぞれどのような内容でしょうか。

In-flight Announcements

1. We will be dimming the cabin lights for take-off, shortly. Your reading light switch can be found in the overhead panel above your seat.

2. Shortly after we reach our cruising altitude, we will commence our in-flight service. We will be serving cocktails and other drinks, followed by dinner.

3. The latest weather information reports clear skies in Honolulu, and a ground temperature of 61 degrees Fahrenheit or 16 degrees Celsius.

4. Please return your seat back, leg rest, and tray table to their original positions and make sure your carry-on luggage is securely stowed in the overhead bins or under the seat in front of you.

5. Those passengers having any fresh fruit, cut flowers, plants, or meat products are requested to go through Plant and Animal Quarantine prior to Customs.

Exercise 3

次の日本語を英語にしましょう。

1. 荷物を下ろすのを手伝っていただけますか？

   _____

2. 枕をもう一つ持って来ていただけないでしょうか。

   _____

3. 免税品の詳細は小冊子をごらんください。

   _____

Chapter ③

Exercise 1

空港到着時の手続き等についてです。どのような内容でしょうか。

1. You must show your passport, arrival card, and explain your purpose for visiting at immigration control.

2. If your suitcase is damaged or missing, you should immediately inform a ground staff.

3. A customs officer may conduct an inspection of passengers' luggage or carry-on bags for any restricted or prohibited items.

4. If you have anything to declare, you must prepare to submit a customs declaration form to the officer and follow his/her instructions.

Exercise 2

次の日本語を英語にしましょう。

1. 海外で英語を勉強する目的は何ですか。

_____

2. ここには英語力を向上させるために来ました。

_____

3. スーツケースをご滞在のところに配達いたします。

_____

Chapter 4

Exercise 1

ホームステイについて，もう少し詳しく学びましょう。

> 1. A student in a homestay gets a private bedroom and is usually provided with breakfast and dinner.
>
> 2. It is strongly advisable for a student to politely ask the host mother or father if he/she has any questions or concerns.
>
> 3. If a student comes home late or eats out, he/she should make sure to inform the host family.
>
> 4. A student is entitled to a consultation with an accommodation officer or homestay coordinator if he/she has any concerns or difficulties with the homestay.

Exercise 2

次の日本語を英語にしましょう。

1. 家事のことでお手数をおかけしまして申し訳ありません。

   _____

2. 私の携帯電話は電池が無くなりかけています。

   _____

3. もし時間があれば，市内を案内します。

   _____

Chapter 5

Exercise 1

日本について，もう少し詳しく学びましょう。

1. Area

   Japan is about 146,000 square miles in area, making it one and a half times larger than the UK and $\frac{1}{25}$ the size of the US.

2. Tokyo

   Tokyo is the capital of Japan with a population of 12,000,000. It is situated at $36°$ north latitude (about the same as Las Vegas in the US), and at $140°$ east longitude (about the same as Adelaide in Australia).

3. Written language

   The Japanese writing system consists of ideograms known as *kanji* and two separate phonetic alphabets called *hiragana* and *katakana*. *Hiragana* and *katakana*, each of which has 48 characters were developed from *kanji*.

4. Kabuki

   Kabuki is one of the most traditional classical arts of Japan dating back to the 17th century. One of its characteristics is that male actors play all the roles.

Exercise 2

次の日本語を英語にしましょう。

1. その地図では小さい点は町を表しています。

   _____

2. 日本人は，ふろしきを昔と同じように使っていますか。

   _____

3. 京都は，西が兵庫で東が滋賀に接しています。

   _____

Chapter 6

Exercise 1

それぞれどういう意味でしょうか。空欄を埋めましょう。

Useful Expressions	役に立つ表現
Excuse me, I am lost.	
How do I get to ...?	
How do you recommend getting to ...?	
How far is it from here?	
Could you tell me where the closest bathroom is?	
Could you call a taxi for us, please?	
Can you take me to this address, please?	
Please let us off over there.	
Is there a bus stop near here/close-by?	

Exercise 2

交通機関を利用する際の留意点や便利表現について，もう少し詳しく学びましょう。

1. If students commute to school using transportation such as buses or trains, they can save money by purchasing a commuter ticket/pass.
2. Concession fares for public transportation are generally available for students.
3. In some cases, buses may be infrequent or run behind schedule, so students should allow themselves plenty of time to get to class.
4. There are also cases where people must hail (raise your arm and wave your hand) the buses themselves, as the buses may not stop otherwise.

Exercise 3

次の日本語を英語にしましょう。

1. このあたりに，列車の駅はありますか。

   _____

2. 一番近い病院はどこか教えてください。

   _____

3. このバスは，エンバーカデロ（Embarcadero）経由で中華街へ行きますか。

   _____

Chapter 7

Exercise 1

語学の研修について，もう少し詳しく学びましょう。

1. Students are evaluated on speaking, listening, reading, writing, homework, and participation in class.

2. Generally, grades are given as follows:
   A - excellent, B - good, C - satisfactory, D - improvement needed or F - fail.

Exercise 2

次の日本語を英語にしましょう。

1. 入学要件についてもう少し説明してください。

_____

2. アメリカで英語を学ぶ目的について簡単に説明します。

_____

3. このプログラムは，ビジネス英語力の開発を目指しています。

_____

Chapter 8

Exercise 1

それぞれどういう意味でしょうか。空欄を埋めましょう。

Useful telephone expressions	役に立つ電話表現
Can/Could I talk/speak to Jack, please?	
Can I speak to the nurse in health services, please?	
Could you connect me to extension 335, please?	
We have a bad connection.	
Could you speak a little louder, please?	
Could you speak a little slower, please?	
I'm sorry, you've got the wrong number.	
I need to talk to someone in customer service.	
I'd like to make a reservation, please.	
He's busy/not available right now/at the moment.	
Can I take a message?	
May I leave a message?	

Exercise 2

次の日本語を英語にしましょう。

1. 私はアメリカの大学院を受験することを考えています。

   _____

2. 道に迷った場合のために，地図を持ち歩いたほうがいいですよ。

   _____

3. 医者に診てもらうためには予約を取らなければならないことを忘れないように，念を押しておきます。

   _____

Exercise 1

それぞれどういう意味でしょうか。空欄を埋めましょう。

Expressions to describe symptoms	病気の状態を表す表現
I have (got) an earache.	
It is hard to breathe.	
I have (got) a runny nose. / My nose is running.	
I have (got) a high fever/temperature.	
I have constipation. / I'm constipated.	
I have (got) heartburn.	
My tooth hurts. / I have a toothache.	
I am allergic to house dust/chemicals.	
I suffer from hay fever.	
My allergies are acting up.	
I have a rash all over my body.	
She has the flu.	
My asthma has subsided	
My eyes are sore. / My eyes are dry.	
I have sprained my left ankle.	
I suffer from anemia.	
I feel run-down/under the weather.	

Exercise 2

病気などの対応についてもう少し詳しく学びましょう。

1. If a student has any chronic conditions such as asthma or diabetes he/she should get permission from his/her doctor to take part in an English program overseas. Also, he/she should have a medical certificate issued in English by his/her doctor in case of emergency.

2. Also, if a student brings any prescription medication overseas, he/she should have a prescription in English from the doctor.

3. In order to be reimbursed for any out-of-pocket medical expenses by an insurance company, students must have the attending doctor's statement and a medical bill issued from the hospital.

Exercise 3

次の日本語を英語にしましょう。

1. お聞きした限りでは，インフルエンザにかかっているようです。

2. 1，2週間ほど家でゆっくりしなさい。

3. 時折，胸に激しい痛みがあります。

Chapter ❿

Exercise 1

次の表現を使って文を作ってみましょう。

Useful Expressions（役に立つ表現）

Introducing your talk
I would like to talk about...
I would like to give a presentation on...
The topic I would like to discuss is...
I am happy to have the chance to speak about...
I am glad to have this opportunity to explain...

Describing graphs and charts
This... describes / explains / indicates / shows...
This... depicts / illustrates / represents...

Exercise 2

プレゼンテーションについて，もう少し詳しく学びましょう。

1. A presentation can have many purposes, such as: to explain, to state opinions, or to persuade.

2. Presentations should not be read. They should be delivered with a strong voice and eye contact.

3. You should always rehearse your presentation before you deliver it.

Exercise 3

次の日本語を英語にしましょう。

1. 将来携わる仕事では，英語力を活かしたいと望んでいます。

   _____

2. この市での公共交通手段について，もう少し詳しく教えてくださいますか。

   _____

3. 環境問題の現状について，皆様に概要を説明します。

   _____

Chapter **11**

Exercise 1

それぞれどういう意味でしょうか。空欄を埋めましょう。

Useful expressions in online meetings	オンラインミーティングでの表現
I have a bad wi-fi connection.	
I was disconnected.	
My connection is unstable.	
I will restart and come back.	
Your microphone is off.	
The sound is breaking up.	
Your sound is echoing.	
Your volume is too low.	
Can you turn the volume up?	
Please mute/unmute your microphone.	
Your screen is frozen.	
Please adjust the angle of your web camera.	
Please open the chat box.	

Exercise 2

下の選択肢から語を選んで，スマートフォン操作やソーシャルメディアでよく使う用語一覧表を完成させましょう。

①受信状態	( ) status
②アプリ	( )
③マナーモード	( ) mode
④通知	( )
⑤月額データ容量制限に達する	reach a monthly data ( )( )
⑥（指操作で）縮小・拡大する	( ) to zoom in/out
⑦SNS	( )( )( )
⑧動画配信サービス	( ) service
⑨インスタ映えする	( )
⑩自撮りする	take a ( )
⑪ネトゲ	( ) game
⑫投稿にイイネ！する	give a ( ) to the post
⑬チャンネル登録してね！	( ) to my channel!

選択肢 app | instagrammable | like | limit | networking | notification | online | pinch | reception | selfie | service | silent | social | streaming | subscribe | usage

Exercise 3

次の日本語を英語にしましょう。

1. 画面の資料を拡大してもらえますか。

_____

2. この講義はライブ配信と，後日のオンデマンド利用のために録画されます。

_____

3. 設定画面で背景画像を簡単に変更できます。

_____

Chapter ⑫

Exercise 1

下は海外のレストランの勘定書の一例です。項目名①〜⑥の日本語の意味を（　　）内に書き入れ，下線部分に金額を計算して書きましょう。

Gourmet Diner
1234 Main Street, New Town
888-888(8888)
www.g*****.com

Order: 11　　　　　　　　　　11/24/20XX
Host: Ashley　　　　　　　　　12:28 PM
Table: 2

2 x Chicken salad bowl @18.95	$ 37.90
1 x Spicy oyster soup	$ 7.25
1 x Fresh orange juice	$ 4.85

① Total Qty (　　　　　): 　4
② Subtotal (　　　　　): 　$ 50.00
③ Sales tax (　　　　) @10% : 　$ _____
④ Local tax (　　　　) @5% : 　$ 2.50
⑤ Gratuity (　　　　): 　$ 8.00
⑥ Total due (　　　　): 　$ _____

Thank you!
Please visit us again.

Exercise 2

下は，食事制限や食文化に関する用語の説明です。あてはまる英単語（1語）をチャプター内から探して（　　）内に書き入れましょう。　※同じ語を2回使う場合もあります。

(1) (　　　　　) are people who choose a lifestyle of eating a plant-based diet, meaning that they do not eat meat or fish. Meanwhile, (　　　　　) people are

those who do not eat eggs, cheese, or milk, in addition to not eating meat and fish, generally because they oppose the use of animals for any purpose.

(2) (   ) foods are foods whose ingredients are prepared and approved by Muslim law. Similarly, (   ) foods are foods allowed under Jewish law. They both help their followers avoid ingredients and cooking methods prohibited for religious reasons. Of course, there are differences between Muslim and Jewish diets. For example, (   ) dietary customs do not allow drinking any alcohol, whereas (   ) dietary customs do allow some alcohol.

(3) Most countries in the world place restrictions on people's drinking, such as drunk driving, (   ) drinking, or drinking in public. However, the rules or laws are different depending on the country. For example, the (   ) age for drinking alcohol is 20 in Japan while it is okay to drink beer at age 16 in Germany. On the other hand, there are also some countries where drinking is not allowed, such as Saudi Arabia.

Exercise 3

それぞれどういう意味でしょうか。空欄を埋めましょう。

Useful expressions at a restaurant	レストランで役に立つ表現
I have a reservation under the name ○○ .	
I am allergic to milk.	
Does this dish have shellfish in it?	
This is a meat-free dish.	
I would like to order this with no mustard.	
What is the specialty here?	
How large is the portion?	
Can I see the menu again?	
Can I have a refill?	
Could you please bring us the check?	
Let's split the bill.	
Could we get separate checks?	
Is the tip already included in the bill?	

Chapter 13

Exercise 1

それぞれどういう意味でしょうか。空欄を埋めましょう。

Expressions for shopping	買い物の表現
I'd like to see the shirt in the window display, please.	
I'm looking for something to go with a blackish jacket.	
I can't figure out my size.	
It's too tight around my hips.	
It's too narrow around my toes.	
Is this belt adjustable?	
Does this need to be hand-washed/dry-cleaned?	
Will the color fade?	
Will it shrink?	
Do you do alterations?	
How much is it all together?	
Here is my credit card.	
Can you give me a discount on this?	
I'd like to exchange this, please?	
Can I get a refund?	

Exercise 2

次の日本語を英語にしましょう。

1. 40代半ばの女性用のプレゼントを探しています。

   _____

2. 茶色でもう少し長めのジャケットはないでしょうか。

   _____

3. あの一番上の棚にある帽子をかぶってみてもいいですか。

   _____

Chapter 14

Exercise 1

それぞれどういう意味でしょうか。空欄を埋めましょう。

Useful Expressions	役に立つ表現
Do you know where the American Airlines counter is?	
How long is the wait at the security check?	
Is the flight on schedule/time?	
How long is the flight?	
Is there Wi-Fi available on this flight?	

Exercise 2

搭乗手続についてもう少し詳しく学びましょう。

1. Please note that luggage to be checked is weighed and inspected at the check-in counter. In most countries, the weight allowance of a suitcase for economy class is 20kg/44 lbs.

2. All passengers are reminded that boarding will commence 30 minutes prior to scheduled departure time.

3. American Airlines flight 22 is now ready for boarding at gate number 5. Would passengers for this flight, please proceed to the boarding area?

Exercise 3

次の日本語を英語にしましょう。

1. 機内の前方で，通路側の席をお願いできますか。

_____

2. 田中ユカが，すでにこの便にチェックインしているかどうか確認してください。

_____

3. このバックパックを手荷物として持ち込みたいのですが。

_____

Chapter 15

書き出しの挨拶（**salutation**）について

男性	女性	
Dear Sir,	Dear Madam,	Formal
Dear Mr. Carter,	Dear Ms. Maclean,	↑
To Whom It May Concern: Dear Dr. Jones, Dear Prof. Smith,		
Dear Tom,	Dear Susan,	↓
Hello Tom,	Hello Susan,	
Hi Tom,	Hi Susan,	Personal

結びの言葉（**complementary close**）について

Sincerely yours,	Formal
Sincerely,	↑
With best regards,	
With best wishes,	
Best regards,	
Best wishes,	
All the best,	↓
Take care!	
Cheers,	Personal

Exercise 1

eメールでは下記のような略語がよく使われます。それぞれどのような表現の略でしょうか。
空欄を埋めましょう。

ASAP	
BTW	
B4	
BRB	
CU	
DM	
FAQ	
FYI	
IMO	
JK	

LMK	
PLS	
TMI	
THX	
TTYL	

Exercise 2

e メールについてもう少し詳しく学びましょう。

Cc stands for carbon copy, and is used to send the same message to people in addition to the original addressee. On the other hand, when a message is sent as bcc (blind carbon copy), the original addressee does not know that the message has been sent to a third person.

Exercise 3

次の日本語を英語にしましょう。

1. アメリカ滞在中の皆様の思いやりに感謝するために手紙を書いております。

   _____

2. 空港で見送っていただいてから，かなりの時間が経ちました。

   _____

3. アメリカの大学で何を専攻するのかに関して，私に何かアドバイスはありますか。

   _____

著者
辻　和成　　　（つじ かずしげ）
辻　勢都　　　（つじ せつ）
田平 真澄　　　（たひら ますみ）
Anita L. Aden　（アニータ・L・エイデン）
Margaret M. Lieb　（マーガレット・M・リーブ）

グローバルキャリアをめざして ［改訂版］
― 留学のためのファーストステップ

2024 年 2 月 20 日　第 1 版発行

編 著 者――辻　和成
　　　　　　辻　勢都
　　　　　　田平 真澄
　　　　　　Anita L. Aden
　　　　　　Margaret M. Lieb

発 行 者――前田 俊秀

発 行 所――株式会社 三修社
　　　　　　〒 150-0001 東京都渋谷区神宮前 2-2-22
　　　　　　TEL03-3405-4511　FAX03-3405-4522
　　　　　　振替 00190-9-72758
　　　　　　https://www.sanshusha.co.jp

印 刷 所――港北メディアサービス株式会社

©2024 Printed in Japan　ISBN978-4-384-33528-6 C1082

編 集 担 当――― 菊池　暁
表紙デザイン――― 岩泉卓屋
本 文 D T P――― 川原田良一
本文イラスト――― キモトケンジ
音 声 録 音――― 一般財団法人 英語教育協議会（ELEC）
音 声 制 作――― 高速録音株式会社